Joey Price understands what it takes to create workplaces where all people thrive. *The Power of HR* is packed with practical advice and real-world insights that can help any HR professional build a great place to work for all. It's a must-read for those ready to make a real impact.
Michael C. Bush, CEO, Great Place to Work

The future of HR and indeed of management depends almost entirely on our ability to persuade top executives that management matters. *The Power of HR* shows us exactly how to make that case. An important and necessary book.
Peter Cappelli, George W. Taylor Professor of Management, The Wharton School

I wish I had had this book in my back pocket as I was growing my HR career. It contains the roadmap that an HR professional should follow to build business-focused people, organizations, and culture strategies and practices that will ensure relevant and impactful outcomes for both organizations and their workforce. The book is both inspirational and practical—full of useful strategies, tools and advice.
Natalie Bickford, Executive Vice-President, Chief People Officer at Sanofi

In *The Power of HR,* Joey Price guides us with insightful narratives and actionable checklists. Joey illustrates HR's potential to drive change, align strategy, foster innovation and, ultimately, create a better world. Whether you're leading a hybrid team or navigating the complexities of DEIB, this book is a masterclass in unlocking HR's strategic power. A must-read for HR professionals ready to shape the future of work.
Enrique Rubio, Founder, Hacking HR

The Power of HR is a groundbreaking exploration of how human resources can drive transformational change in organizations. This book expertly combines forward-thinking strategies with practical insights, making it an essential guide for HR professionals who want to shape the future of work. A must-read for anyone looking to elevate HR's role as a strategic force for innovation, growth and people-centric leadership.

Dan Schawbel, Managing Partner of Workplace Intelligence

Talent management thought leader Joey Price himself said it best: HR leaders are the architects of the new world of work. *The Power of HR* is an essential blueprint chock full of case studies, exercises and scenarios to get the job done and build your own career and reputation in the process.

Alexandra Levit, author of *Deep Talent*

The Power of HR is one of the best books for HR leaders looking to make a lasting impact. Joey Price delivers practical advice, real-world examples, and actionable tools to help HR professionals lead with confidence and purpose. This book is a game-changer for anyone serious about elevating their career.

Laurie Ruettimann, Author and HR Consultant

Joey Price has an incredible way of making complex HR challenges feel manageable and even exciting. *The Power of HR* feels like sitting down with a trusted mentor—one who genuinely understands the realities of today's workplace. Joey's advice is approachable, practical and packed with insights that will stick with you long after you've finished the book.

Sarah White, CEO and Founder, Aspect 43

The Power of HR

*How to Make an Organizational Impact
as a People Professional*

Joey Price

KoganPage

First published in Great Britain and the United States in 2025 by Kogan Page Limited

Kogan Page
Kogan Page Ltd, 2nd Floor, 45 Gee Street, London EC1V 3RS, United Kingdom
Kogan Page Inc, 8 W 38th Street, Suite 90, New York, NY 10018, USA
www.koganpage.com

EU Representative (GPSR)
Authorised Rep Compliance Ltd, Ground Floor, 71 Lower Baggot Street, Dublin D02 P593, Ireland
www.arccompliance.com

Kogan Page books are printed on paper from sustainable forests.

ISBNs
Hardback   9781398618978
Paperback   9781398618954
Ebook   9781398618961

British Library Cataloguing-in-Publication Data
A CIP record for this book is available from the British Library.

Library of Congress Control Number
2025930266

Typeset by Hong Kong FIVE Workshop
Print production managed by Jellyfish
Printed and bound by CPI Group (UK) Ltd, Croydon, CR0 4YY

CONTENTS

ACKNOWLEDGMENTS

I'd like to dedicate this book to my wife Candace and our beautiful daughters Jordan and Parker. You continue to be a source of love, inspiration, and encouragement. I'd like to also dedicate this book to my parents Vincent and Dorothy, who always believed that the little kid who loved to read would one day go on to do great things. Lastly, I want to acknowledge every mentor and colleague who has helped shape the professional I've become. While there are too many to name, if you are reading this and believe you're on the list—you're probably right!

UNLOCK ADDITIONAL RESOURCES ONLINE

Your journey to making an organizational impact doesn't end with the pages of this book. We've created an exclusive online hub packed with resources to help you dive deeper and make the most of *The Power of HR*.

What you'll find

For Educators

Comprehensive teaching guides, discussion prompts, and case study materials to enhance your HR courses.

For HR Professionals

Practical tools, templates, and extended insights to implement strategies and frameworks from the book in your workplace.

Visit now

www.joeyvpricehr.com/power or use the QR code.

Whether you're shaping future HR leaders or driving change in your organization, these resources are here to support you every step of the way. Check it out today!

Introduction:
The Power of HR in the
New World of Work

The business world is transforming at an unprecedented pace. New technologies, shifting workforce dynamics, and evolving social and political landscapes are rewriting the rules for success at both organizational and professional levels. In the midst of this chaos, organizations that hope to stay competitive must adapt—or risk being left behind. As the workforce changes, so too must the approach to managing it. And no function within a company is more critical to leading that charge than Human Resources.

Too often, HR has been viewed as a back-office, administrative role that merely handles tasks like payroll, recruitment, and employee discipline. But that perception is outdated, dangerous, and limiting. The truth is that HR has the potential to be the most strategic department in any organization, touching every aspect of business performance and success. This book, *The Power of HR*, will show you how to unlock that potential. HR professionals must position themselves as the architects of the modern workforce, navigating the complexities of a new era. This book isn't just an addition to your library—it's the key to thriving in today's workplace.

In this book, we will explore why HR is at the center of business success and why you, as an HR professional, are uniquely equipped to lead your organization into the future.

The Urgent Need for HR to Embrace Change

A Competitive Edge in a Changing World

Organizations that fail to adapt to the evolving work environment are doomed to lose momentum and relevance. The challenge of hiring, developing, and retaining a productive workforce is more complex than ever. Traditional methods of workforce management simply don't work in a world where employees value purpose, culture, and flexibility over stability. The sociopolitical climate has changed how people evaluate potential employers and organizations that do not recognize this shift will struggle to attract the talent they need to thrive.

HR professionals are uniquely positioned to lead this transformation. But to do so, we must rethink our roles and responsibilities. We are not just gatekeepers of policies—we are the stewards of company culture, the drivers of employee engagement, and the architects of workforce strategy.

As you read through this book, remember: organizations that are unwilling or unable to adapt will fall behind. HR professionals who understand the changing landscape will not only survive but thrive.

Why HR Is the Key to Success

No other function in an organization is as well prepared to address these challenges as HR. In fact, HR is the only department with the ability to influence people, processes, and brand reputation all at once. HR touches every aspect of an organization, from the hiring process to the development of team members, to fostering a company culture that aligns with brand values.

HR empowers organizations to:

- attract, develop, and retain a high-performing workforce
- navigate complex business processes that require accountability and collaboration

- ensure alignment between brand promises and the people hired to fulfill them

A company can create the most innovative products or have the clearest vision, but without the right people in place, none of that will matter. HR is the key to making sure those people are not only in place but are positioned to thrive.

HR's Five Guiding Principles: Unlocking Your Full Potential

Over the course of my HR career, I've identified five guiding principles that every HR professional should adopt to maximize their influence and effectiveness. These principles are not just theoretical—they're practical strategies that I've seen work time and time again. As you move forward in your career, remember that these principles are the foundation of what it means to truly unleash the power of HR.

1. Own Your Expertise

The modern workplace is complex. Executive leadership is grappling with challenges it has never faced before, from the rise of hybrid work models to increasing demands for corporate social responsibility. As an HR leader, your first superpower is your wisdom—wisdom in areas that no one else in the organization may fully understand.

The challenges facing organizations today often come down to human performance, labor compliance, and organizational strategy. HR professionals are uniquely positioned to understand these intersections and offer solutions. This is where your expertise shines. You are the expert on human capital, and it's time to own that expertise unapologetically.

In later chapters, we'll dive deeper into specific disciplines where HR leaders must excel, but for now, understand this: your voice is essential in the boardroom because you bring a perspective that no one else can offer.

2. Be Part Coach, Part Cheerleader

One of the most powerful roles you can play as an HR leader is that of both a coach and a cheerleader. Great coaches assess performance, identify areas for improvement, and help individuals and teams make the necessary adjustments. Cheerleaders, on the other hand, provide the encouragement and motivation teams need to push through challenges.

As an HR professional, you must strike the right balance between these two roles. You have an obligation to tell the truth, even when it's hard. But remember that truth is best received when delivered with optimism. Building trust with employees and leadership will make your feedback more impactful, and your ability to inspire others will keep the team moving forward.

3. Ignite the Spark

In the current work environment, HR leaders must inspire confidence and trust. Whether you're facing a hiring shortage, a challenge with diversity and inclusion, or navigating through a crisis like racial inequity investigations, your ability to inspire trust is crucial. HR leaders who can ignite the spark of confidence will earn their place as trusted advisors and valued partners in organizational success.

Another aspect of this principle is ensuring that leadership and staff alike see HR as a strategic partner. You are not just there to enforce rules; you're there to help the company achieve its goals by building the right teams and fostering the right culture.

4. Bring Clarity From the Clouds

The Covid-19 pandemic threw businesses into a state of uncertainty. It was HR that often led the way in bringing clarity. Whether it was designing new safety protocols or creating communication strategies to keep teams connected, HR played a vital role in ensuring business continuity.

Bringing clarity in uncertain times is one of HR's most important responsibilities. Your organization relies on you to provide clear, actionable steps that help the business move forward, even in the face of chaos.

The modern workplace will continue to present unpredictable challenges. As an HR leader, your role is to help bring clarity from the clouds, ensuring your organization can navigate the unknown with confidence.

5. Forward and Adaptive Beats Static and Slow

The pace of business today is faster than ever. With the rise of artificial intelligence (AI), machine learning (ML), and new technologies, organizations must be agile and forward-thinking. As an HR leader, you must embrace this pace.

This doesn't mean rushing into decisions—it means being ready to adapt and move as quickly as the business environment demands. If you wait too long, you risk being left behind. Forward and adaptive leadership will set you apart from those who remain static and slow. The world is moving fast—HR leaders must move with it.

Key Competencies for the Modern HR Professional

The five principles discussed above provide a strong foundation, but to truly excel, the modern HR professional needs a few critical competencies. These skills will allow you to effectively influence both leadership and employees, helping you navigate the complex challenges of today's workforce. They are the foundation for the five values you've just read about above.

Business Acumen

HR is no longer just about people—it's about understanding the business as a whole. To be truly effective, you must have a deep understanding of how your organization operates, including its finances, strategic goals, and operational challenges. This business acumen allows you to speak the language of executives and position HR as a key driver of business success.

Empathetic Leadership

In a diverse workforce, empathy is critical. Empathy isn't just about caring for others—it's about guiding them with compassion. The modern HR leader must be able to navigate a variety of viewpoints, beliefs, and experiences with grace and understanding.

Infectious Trustworthiness

Your reputation is everything. HR leaders must manage their personal brand alongside the organization's brand. Trustworthiness is essential, not just in formal settings like board meetings but in everyday interactions with employees.

Transformational Problem-Solving

Today's business problems are complex, and HR is often at the center of solving them. From handling workplace conflicts to implementing diversity initiatives, HR leaders must approach these challenges with a problem-solving mindset that transforms obstacles into opportunities.

Proactive Communication

In today's fast-paced world, decisions must be made quickly, and communication must be proactive. HR leaders need to provide timely feedback and ensure that their communication meets the needs of the moment. Being forward-thinking in your communication strategy will ensure you stay ahead of potential problems.

HR's Role in Shaping the Future

As HR leaders, we are responsible for helping our organizations navigate the modern world of work. Technology will play a significant role, but it's important to remember that technology alone cannot solve every problem. Tools need human insight and context to be effective, and that's where HR comes in.

Additionally, businesses cannot succeed with a "management by the numbers" approach. Profit and loss statements may reflect the financial health of a company, but they do not capture the human element that drives success. HR's role is to ensure that the people behind the numbers are engaged, motivated, and supported.

Organizations that cling to traditional HR practices are at risk of becoming obsolete. Modern HR leaders must be forward-thinking, adaptive, and innovative.

How This Book Will Help You Harness the Power of HR

The world of HR is evolving, and to be at the forefront, you need a clear roadmap that not only explains why HR is key to business success but also provides the tools and strategies to thrive as an HR leader. That's exactly what this book is designed to offer. From the first page to the last, I've structured this book to be both informative and practical, ensuring you can apply what you learn as you go.

The book is divided into two key sections.

Part 1: Understanding the Business Case for the Power of HR

The first half of this book lays the foundation by walking you through the business case for HR's indispensable role in organizational success. It's not just about getting HR a seat at the table—it's about understanding why HR is the key driver of success in today's competitive environment.

We will explore how HR impacts areas such as company culture, talent acquisition, performance management, and leadership development. Throughout these chapters, I'll share reflections, real-world case studies, and helpful insights that will energize you to become a transformative HR leader. My goal is to equip you with a clear understanding of why HR is more critical than ever and how you can position yourself as the driving force behind your company's growth.

This section also challenges some of the outdated views of HR, reframing the function as a strategic powerhouse rather than an administrative necessity. By the end of this first half, you'll have a thorough understanding of how HR can—and must—become a vital partner in your organization's long-term success.

Part 2: A Blueprint for HR's Unique Impact

The second half of the book builds on the first by providing you with actionable strategies for making a real difference in your organization. Here, we dive into key areas that HR uniquely influences, such as navigating sociopolitical complexities, fostering inclusion and equity, managing remote and hybrid teams, and shaping a forward-thinking talent strategy. This section serves as a blueprint, giving you the practical tools and mindset needed to address the challenges of the modern workforce.

What sets this part of the book apart is its focus on future-ready HR strategies. We'll explore how to stay ahead of the curve by leveraging new technologies, adapting to shifts in employee expectations, and fostering a culture of innovation. With these insights, you'll be prepared to not just survive but thrive in today's rapidly changing business environment.

Enhancing the Value You Get Out of This Book

This book isn't just about reading concepts—it's about putting them into practice. That's why each section is designed to deliver maximum value with a variety of tools and resources that will enhance your learning experience. Let me walk you through how this structure will work.

RELATABLE STORIES

Each chapter opens with a fictional, yet relatable, story that sets the tone for the lessons you'll discover. These stories reflect common challenges HR professionals face, helping you immediately see yourself in the situations. Whether it's navigating a crisis, dealing with a difficult leadership team, or managing the cultural dynamics of a diverse workforce, these stories are crafted to be both engaging and thought-provoking.

A MODERN MINDSET

After setting the stage with the story, I'll explain the modern HR mindset needed to stand out as a truly impactful leader. HR in today's world requires agility, empathy, and strategic thinking. In this section, I'll break down how you can cultivate these qualities, shift outdated perspectives, and adopt a forward-thinking approach to HR leadership.

REFLECTIONS AND GUIDANCE

I've been fortunate to learn from some of the most respected professionals in the HR world. In each chapter, you'll find reflections and guidance from both myself and several mentors who have made significant contributions to the field. These individuals have been on the cutting edge of powerful HR leadership in their respective organizations, and their insights will offer you practical wisdom and inspiration for your own journey.

OVERCOMING ROADBLOCKS

Let's be honest—HR leadership isn't without its challenges. That's why each chapter includes a section dedicated to identifying potential roadblocks and offering strategies to overcome them. Whether it's dealing with resistance to change, managing conflicting priorities, or building influence with the C-suite, I'll share tips and tactics for navigating these obstacles successfully.

CASE STUDIES

To help you connect theory with real-world application, each chapter includes a fictional scenario that mirrors actual challenges I've encountered during my HR career. These case studies will allow you to think critically about how to apply what you've learned to similar situations in your own organization. They're educational exercises designed to challenge your thinking and prepare you for what's to come.

PRESCRIPTIVE CHECKLISTS

Finally, each chapter closes with a prescriptive checklist of tips and action items that can serve as a performance review or check-in as you learn and implement new skills. These checklists are practical tools that can guide you in assessing your progress, reflecting on what you've learned and applying it to your daily work. Use these checklists as part of your personal development plan or share them with your HR team to drive collective progress.

A Book You'll Return to Again and Again

My goal in writing this book is not just for you to read it once and move on. I've designed it to be a resource you'll return to throughout your career. Whether you're facing a new challenge, need a boost of inspiration, or simply want to refresh your knowledge, this book will serve as your go-to guide.

Conclusion: The Power of HR in Your Hands

As an HR leader, you have the unique opportunity to shape the future of your organization. You have the power to influence people, processes, and brand reputation in ways no other function can. This book is your companion on that journey, offering the strategies, insights, and tools you need to make a lasting impact.

As you progress through these chapters, remember that the world of HR is ever-changing. Stay adaptable, stay informed, and stay committed to your role as a transformative leader. The power of HR is not just in its ability to manage people—it's in its ability to drive the success of an entire organization. And that's a power worth mastering.

Let's get to work.

PART 1

Understanding the Business Case for the Power of HR

1

Why HR Is Key to Business Success

Introduction

Human Resources has often been perceived as the function that sits on the sidelines, managing processes but never truly leading the charge. That perception is outdated and severely underestimates the power of HR. In today's rapidly changing business landscape, the HR function is more vital than ever, shaping not only how companies hire and retain employees but how they navigate crises, manage performance, and develop future leaders. The time for HR to step up and drive business success is now.

As HR professionals, we possess a unique vantage point—we see the pulse of the workforce and understand how to align human capital with business goals. This chapter is about recognizing that HR is not just about compliance, payroll, or employee benefits. HR is about leading change, influencing leadership decisions, and shaping a company's culture to drive sustained success. By aligning our efforts with the organization's broader goals, managing talent effectively, and fostering employee engagement, we can transform HR into the strategic powerhouse it was always meant to be.

The case study in this chapter serves as a testament to the transformative power of HR. Whether you're tackling challenges related to performance management, employee morale, or leadership alignment, this is your opportunity to bring real value to the table. Your ability to lead and influence from an HR perspective can—and will—drive the success of your entire organization.

"What Do You Do for a Living?"

Have you ever tried to explain what it is you do for a living at a dinner party? Sure, the answer is "I work in HR," but what does that really mean? We're not quite finance professionals—but we process payroll, calculate labor projections, and manage organization-wide budgets for training and development. We're not legal professionals, but we keep CEOs out of jail and companies out of the news by ensuring that our organizations follow the law and stay compliant as the legal and political landscape evolves. We're not marketing professionals, but we hire, recruit, and retain our workforce using employer branding tactics that rival the best marketing campaigns out there. We're not IT professionals, but we are a business function that is increasingly responsible for navigating the intersection of the world of work and robots and adapting to a world full of remote workforce management, artificial intelligence, and fast-evolving HR technology. So what are we, again?

Let's take a look at a realistic example of the power HR has in a business and the influence strategic mentors can play in shaping your career.

The Tale of Transformation: An HR Hero's Journey

In the bustling city that never sleeps, Sarah Jennings, a seasoned HR director at Techtonic Innovations—a company teetering on the brink of chaos—found herself at a crossroads.

Techtonic, once a market leader, was faltering. Stock prices had plummeted, morale was at a low, and the departure of key talents had become a routine headline in the industry's newsletters. Just this morning, another meeting with the company's CEO, who was blissfully unaware of the toxic environment their leadership style had cultivated, had pushed Sarah to her limit.

Her phone buzzed with a notification. It was an email from me about a webinar happening that afternoon titled "Resilient HR: Leading Change in Turbulent Times." On impulse, Sarah decided to attend, hoping for a sign that might sway her decision.

The webinar was transformative for her. I stood outlining how HR could be the linchpin in turning a failing company around. I talked about creating a vibrant workforce vision, building a culture that thrives on challenge, and implementing a people management strategy that aligns closely with the company's core objectives. Each was presented through a methodical business case that outlined why each pillar was important to the overall goal of effective change management.

Inspired, Sarah contacted me and I agreed to meet her the following day. Over coffee, I leaned in and listened closely as Sarah painted a bleak picture of Techtonic.

"Sarah, remember, in every crisis lies great opportunity. Your role is pivotal. You are the bridge between the workforce and upper management. You can lead this change, not by overturning the boardroom but by steering it gently towards more self-aware leadership and a more engaged workforce. Think about what changes you can make that align with your values and the company's mission. Think about the business case."

My words struck a chord. Sarah realized that her deep understanding of the company's workforce and her commitment to their wellbeing were not just a part of her job—they were her calling.

Reinvigorated, Sarah returned to work with a new perspective. She started small, organizing workshops fostering communication between employees and executives and advocating for policies prioritizing employee welfare. Each win was achieved through convincing internal stakeholders that the business case for change was not a luxury but an imperative. Gradually, the atmosphere at Techtonic began to change. Employees started to engage more, productivity increased, and, slowly, the company clawed its way back from the edge of despair.

Six months later, as Sarah prepared for Techtonic's annual general meeting, she reflected on her journey. She hadn't just saved her career, she had transformed a company's culture and redirected its path to success.

As she walked onto the stage to present the changes and their impressive results, she felt a surge of pride. Her story was a testament to the power of HR in shaping not just a company's future but also its people's lives.

Sarah posed a question that resonated with the room, filled with intrigued stakeholders and executives: "If HR is the key to unlocking organizational potential, what are we waiting for to turn the key and open more doors to success?"

This question not only marked the beginning of a new chapter for Techtonic, it also challenged each person present to think about the role of HR in a new, transformative light.

This sets the stage for the profound discussions that will populate the rest of this book.

Essential HR: Building the Business Case

"The value of a business is a function of how well the financial capital and intellectual capital are managed by human capital. You'd better get the human capital part right."—Dave Bookbinder

Building a strong business case for HR initiatives is a powerful way to secure trust from the C-suite and demonstrate your strategic value to employees. It is a powerful discipline you will need to master for not just long-range planning but when evaluating the merit on shorter-term initiatives as well.

In today's ever-changing business environment, HR professionals must be able to present clear, data-driven arguments that showcase the impact of their initiatives on the organization's success. Gone are the days where you could simply plan out an HR calendar and run the same plays year after year siloed apart from other key performance measures within the organization. Leaders and employees alike now understand that the HR department is the connective tissue that influences every part of the business. When the HR function is thriving, businesses succeed. However, when the HR function is suboptimal, you may experience breakdowns in performance, talent attraction, employee engagement, and other areas. This is not just talk, this is truth. In an article from Gallup (Harter, 2024), the international workforce research organization revealed the results of its annual poll on employee engagement. In the survey they found that only 33 percent of employees were engaged, and this lack of engagement resulted in $1.9 trillion in lost productivity (Harter, 2024). If this snapshot is any indication of our ability to create healthy workplaces, there is a lot to be desired. But there's hope! And part of that hope is understanding that agility, analysis, and action are the core competencies that we must introduce as we live and work in this ever-changing society.

When we look at defining the parameters of what counts as HR and what drives positive engagement, we have to expand our scope. In a post-Covid-19 workforce, several new aspects of work have become firmly planted in the purview of HR:

- mental wellness and neurodiversity inclusion
- workplace safety and sanitization
- workplace location management (think in-person, hybrid, or fully remote)
- artificial intelligence's impact on workforce planning
- gig workers' roles, responsibilities, and rights
- the influence of a vocal Gen Z on the workplace

And so much more...

As senior HR professionals, understanding how to build a compelling business case is an essential component to our success. It enhances our credibility, influences corporate decision-making, and aligns our initiatives with the broader business goals. As you continue to read this chapter, you will not only explore the key components and steps necessary to create a robust business case that resonates with leadership, you will also gain access to expert mentorship and thought leadership that is filled with research and practical applications.

What Is a Business Case?

Before jumping into how to develop a business case, we must first have a shared agreement on what the phrase means. Otherwise, it is impossible to find unity and agreement as we go deeper into the text.

A business case is a formal, structured document—or argument— that outlines the justification for a specific initiative or project. It includes a thorough analysis of the costs, benefits, risks, and alignment with organizational goals. The primary purpose is to provide decision-makers with the necessary information to make an informed judgment. For example, let's say your CEO has decided they want every employee to return to the office five days a week within 30 days or face termination. It is understood that many critical employees have relocated away from the office when operations went fully remote, and you also know that your CEO is not aware that you've had to create new tax accounts for several states because your employees relocated during the pandemic.

What do you do? Do you simply give in to the demands of your CEO and risk the mass turnover, or do you compile your thoughts and data points to help persuade your CEO to consider changing their position? This is where the business case comes in.

Why Is a Business Case Important?

Why is building a business case essential for HR? It's simple. In order to influence the world of business you have to be able to speak its language. As HR professionals, we often stand out amongst our corporate peers in terms of our soft skills, ability to connect via emotional intelligence, and to think of the personnel factors of strategic initiatives that get lost or deprioritized when we're not at the table. But the need for powerful HR in our organizations is far too great for us to sit on the sidelines or not grow in this skill. There are three core reasons why business cases are an important tool to add to our toolkit.

Firstly, it allows us to clearly articulate the value of our initiatives. When you give yourself an opportunity to get your thoughts on paper, it helps you sort through which ideas are strong and which ones are not. By strong, I mean which ideas will influence, and by weak, I mean which ideas will not resonate. Before giving your CEO your opinion, you must understand the arguments and data points that will be most convincing and that comes with understanding the priorities of your CEO as much as you understand the drivers of employee engagement. When you draft your argument, what should you say about team morale? What is the dollar value associated with changing policies or allowing them to remain the same? What are the legal ramifications?

If you want to be a powerful people leader, you have to first be able to construct a position that holds weight, influence, and value to the person you want to agree with you. And even if you find yourself taking a position that sides with your leader, being able to justify how and why you've arrived at your own conclusions helps leadership know that you stand competent in areas that matter most to the discussion.

Secondly, knowing how to develop a business case provides a framework for evaluating the potential return on investment of an initiative or position. Let's say that the CEO is looking to bring employees back to the office because the cost of the office lease cannot be justified with all staff not reporting to the office with some regularity. Help your CEO reach the best return on investment by thinking through not just the financial ramifications of a decision but also the legal ramifications, employee morale ramifications, and public sentiment ramifications. As easy as it is to understand the cost of a lease, you might also find that other critical pieces may or may not need to be weighed as heavily as cash.

When you have a repeatable framework for developing your position, you can take comfort in the fact that you will create a position that takes as many factors into consideration as possible while understanding what key priorities exist in decision-making.

Lastly, it ensures that our proposals are aligned with the strategic objectives of the organization, thereby increasing the likelihood of approval and support. Can I tell you one of the fastest ways to lose the confidence of your CEO? By advocating strongly for policies, procedures, and positions that are at odds with the strategic objectives of the organization. It makes you seem unsure at best and counter-culture at worst. This is not an issue that is unique to HR, but it's one we must be sure to guard ourselves against. I remember sitting with the CEO of a client organization that we had just started supporting. We were a few months into the working relationship and the CEO mentioned that they felt comfortable with me and had high trust in me because they knew that I cared about what they cared about. One reason for that happening so quickly was because I made a point to understand the organization, what mission it set out to accomplish, and I understood the CEO's dedication to see the mission matter above everything else. You don't want to appear counterproductive to an organization's mission.

Key Components of a Strong Business Case

Here are my recommendations for building a strong business case. The context of your circumstances and staff support may be different, but this information will be helpful the next time you want to craft more powerful business cases surrounding HR issues.

SET CLEAR OBJECTIVES
The first step in building a business case is to define clear and measurable objectives. What are you trying to achieve? What is the greatest outcome desired under ideal circumstances? Whether it's improving employee engagement, reducing turnover, or enhancing leadership development, our goals must be specific, measurable, achievable, relevant, and time-bound (SMART). For example, if your objective is to improve employee engagement, then you should aim to increase engagement scores by a certain percentage within a defined timeframe.

A clear position is also not a wavering one. A major part of setting clear objectives is to pick a side. When you are in a position of leadership, you are either moving towards something or standing still. Effective leadership does not stand still.

WEIGH THE COST-BENEFIT ANALYSIS

The next step would be to conduct a thorough cost-benefit analysis. This involves identifying all the costs associated with the initiative, including direct, indirect, and opportunity costs. We then compare these costs to the anticipated benefits. This comparison should be presented in both quantitative and qualitative terms. For instance, if we are proposing a new training program, we should calculate the expected increase in productivity and the potential reduction in turnover. These calculations then become core metrics to gauge an initiative's success.

You may be someone reading this book who says "I'm not a numbers person," or "I didn't get into HR to do math. If I wanted to do math, I would have been an accountant." To that I would say—I hear you! In fact, prior to obtaining my Master's in Human Resources Management in 2011, I would have agreed with you. But alas, the language of business is in fact finance. Your ability to master storytelling through numbers will be a key that unlocks many doors for you. Unlock the next level of your professional career by coupling emotional intelligence with financial acumen. I encourage you to take a Financial Management for Managers class if talking in terms of return on investment (ROI) and budgets is an unfamiliar or intimidating subject. This is a helpful way to not only gain a seat at the executive table but be fluent in the conversations that happen there.

EVALUATE THE RISK

A comprehensive business case also includes a risk assessment. What are the potential risks associated with the initiative, and how can they be mitigated? Identifying these risks upfront and developing strategies to address them demonstrates thorough planning and enhances credibility. Risk is not always solely legal or financial. There may be times where there are factors such as morale, team dynamics, employee experience, candidate experience or other important considerations that must be identified.

One such example of risk mitigation (where I was negatively impacted) occurred in my professional HR career just before I started my firm. I had been hired on to a local company in my home state to serve as an HR specialist and heir apparent to become the HR Director. In the interview process, I was praised for hitting all the key items: a Master's Degree, I had passed the PHR certification test, and experience over the years prior made me a great candidate. Was I naive, in hindsight, in not asking why I was only interviewing with the co-founders of the business and not the HR Director? Perhaps, but the story continues.

After a period of several months, I realized that there had been an incumbent HR Director who was out under the Family Medical Leave Act (FMLA). I had always assumed that this individual would not be returning to work and that as soon as she resigned, a clear path to leadership would open up for me. I couldn't have been more wrong. As time passed, I was met with a conversation that no professional wants to hear. And it went something like this: "We have to let you go."

While I was hurt and immediately worried about my future, hindsight brought clarity for me. At the time, I was in my mid-twenties and on the upswing of my career. The HR Director at the time was a member of several protected classes and to terminate them would have opened up the risk of a retaliation claim for needing the leave in the first place. There's an old saying that goes "You can't have two cooks in the kitchen," and that is when I soon decided to open up my own shop.

I never looked back at the firm over the years to see how they've been performing or if the HR Director is still there, but the valuable lesson here is that your business case has to account for risk mitigation. Sometimes it will present competing priorities but it is your ethical obligation to outline the risk and create a plan to move forward with as little risk as possible.

STRATEGIC ALIGNMENT

Finally, we must ensure that our initiative aligns with the broader organizational goals. This means understanding the company's strategic objectives and demonstrating how our proposal supports these objectives. For instance, if the organization is focused on innovation, we can highlight how our initiative fosters a culture of continuous learning and development, which is essential for innovation.

Strategic alignment represents the cornerstone of a persuasive business case for many reasons. Those reasons include organizational fit, persuasive argument, and collaborative appeal. Let's unpack these one by one.

Organizational fit would best be described as an idea or plan of action that feels authentic to the values, mission, and strategy of the organization. Values are important to honor because the idea must be able to reflect the chosen set of beliefs that employees have about working there. If you are pitching ideas for cost-cutting measures, do you start with layoffs or do you peel back benefits? If you are looking to improve candidate experience, do you hire more recruiting coordinators or do you implement new automation technology? These are some of the questions that have a lot to do with organizational fit.

Persuasive arguments are positions that help the hearer become more convinced and believe in the position they're listening to. This is incredibly important when advocating for yourself and for your department initiatives. Not every stakeholder will see things the way you do, but perhaps they should. In order to ensure your business case is persuasive, think about the following things:

- Who is my audience?
- What do they care about?
- What objections might they have?
- What longstanding beliefs do they have that I might have to acknowledge and account for in my discussion?
- Why am I confident in my position point?

Collaborative appeal is when your business case incorporates various sources and voices in your presentation. Collaboration is important because it is harder to build a business case alone than it is to do so when you know you've earned or sought the support of stakeholders before you've gone public with your case.

One of the best ways to think about the value of collaboration is to look at the process by which we introduce and pass legislation in a typical city. Very rarely does a request become a mandate without collaboration and buy-in from idea to execution. Perhaps an angry citizen wants parking signs placed on their street because residents have to compete for parking spaces with visitors who come for the local bars and restaurants. The angry citizen canvases the neighborhood for signatures in support of this initiative and they find 50 percent of the neighbors to sign their request. From that point, they speak with their City Council representative and petition for something to be done on their street.

The City Council representative realizes that it's an election year and they would do well to appease their voting base so they consult the City's Public Works department and commission a study. After the study comes back in favor of the citizens who live on the street, new parking signs go up. Without collaboration, it's hard to build momentum, advocacy, and a group of people who will champion your cause as if it were their own. In fact, you want as many people as possible to believe your business case is the best way to benefit their goals.

Steps for Building the Business Case

Data Collection and Analysis

Start by gathering relevant data to support your business case. This data can come from internal sources such as employee surveys, performance metrics, and financial reports, as well as external sources such as industry benchmarks and best practices. Analyze this data to identify trends, gaps, and opportunities. For example, if employee turnover is high, analyze exit interview data to identify common reasons for leaving.

Stakeholder Engagement

Engage key stakeholders early in the process to gain insights and support. This includes executives, managers, and employees who will be affected by the initiative. Conducting interviews, focus groups, and workshops can help gather valuable input and build buy-in.

For example, involving department heads in the planning process can ensure that the initiative addresses their specific needs and concerns.

Developing the Proposal

Craft a clear and compelling proposal that outlines the initiative's value. This should include an executive summary, the problem statement, proposed solution, cost-benefit analysis, risk assessment, and implementation plan. Use visual aids such as charts and graphs to enhance clarity and impact. For example, a well-designed infographic can effectively illustrate the anticipated ROI of the initiative.

Presenting the Business Case

Present your business case to decision-makers in a structured and persuasive manner. Highlight the key points and focus on the strategic value of the initiative. Be prepared to answer questions and address concerns. Effective presentation techniques, such as storytelling and real-life examples, can help engage the audience and make a stronger impact. For instance, sharing a success story from another organization that implemented a similar initiative can illustrate the potential benefits.

In summary, building a strong business case for HR initiatives involves defining clear objectives, conducting a thorough cost-benefit analysis, assessing risks, and ensuring strategic alignment. It also requires collecting and analyzing relevant data, engaging stakeholders, developing a clear proposal, and presenting it effectively to decision-makers.

As HR professionals, we must prioritize building strong business cases to secure the support needed to drive our initiatives. By doing so, we can demonstrate our strategic value and contribute to the overall success of our organizations. Remember, a compelling business case is not just a document, it's a tool for strategic influence.

Mentor's Corner: Redefining HR's Strategic Role and Lessons from Dave Ulrich on Outside/In Leadership

When I thought about writing this book, I wanted to pay homage to innovative HR leaders who inspire my thought and practice of the field of HR. There is no stronger voice, in my opinion, than that of Dave Ulrich.

In this segment of Mentor's Corner, the goal is for you to have a deeper understanding of how HR professionals must evolve to truly drive business success. One key takeaway from our discussion was the distinction between strategic alignment and what Dave calls the "outside/in" perspective. Strategic alignment, as Dave explains, focuses on how HR helps achieve a company's goals, much like looking in a mirror where the focus is internal—mobilizing talent, performance management, and resource allocation based on the CEO's direction. While this has been a traditional HR strength, it only addresses part of the equation.

The outside/in perspective, on the other hand, shifts the focus outward. It's about looking through the window, assessing how customers and shareholders perceive the organization in real-time. It demands that HR not only support internal strategies but also be responsive to how the business performs against external expectations. This is where the real power of HR lies—making agile adjustments based on real-world outcomes, rather than just organizational aspirations.

In practical terms, Dave shared examples of companies that design leadership development programs in collaboration with customers to ensure that what leaders learn is directly relevant to delivering customer value. HR professionals must see themselves not only as facilitators of employee experience but as key players in enhancing customer satisfaction and investor confidence. By aligning employee commitment and development with what customers truly want, HR can significantly enhance stakeholder value.

Applying the Five HR Values in Alignment with Dave Ulrich's Perspective

Let's now explore how the five core HR values can be applied to the concepts Dave is famous for, ensuring HR professionals can thrive in the modern workforce.

OWN YOUR EXPERTISE

Owning your expertise is about recognizing that HR professionals possess unique knowledge in areas like human performance, compliance, and talent strategy. This expertise should not be confined to internal organizational goals, but should extend to the external marketplace. In alignment with Dave's outside/in perspective, owning your expertise means being confident in HR's ability to influence how the organization performs for its customers and shareholders.

Practical example: Consider an HR leader at a retail company. Owning their expertise would involve not just improving internal customer service training but understanding how external customers perceive the brand. By incorporating customer feedback into training programs, HR ensures that employees are equipped to meet customer expectations, directly impacting customer satisfaction and loyalty.

BE PART COACH, PART CHEERLEADER

One thing Dave shared with me was that HR must be responsive to real-time performance of the organization. Being part coach, part cheerleader is key to that responsiveness. HR professionals should guide their teams with the truth, offering course corrections when necessary, while also maintaining a positive and supportive environment that encourages engagement and growth.

Practical example: In a tech company struggling with employee retention, HR could act as a coach by identifying gaps in the employee experience that are contributing to turnover—whether that's lack of career development opportunities or misaligned job expectations. At the same time, HR can cheerlead by recognizing and celebrating small wins, such as increased engagement from employees who participate in new professional development programs. This approach creates a culture where employees feel both supported and guided toward improvement. Take this one step further and track the correlation between professional development and sales outcomes to show the power that HR has in the organization.

IGNITE THE SPARK

Confidence and trust are critical in the HR role, as Dave emphasizes. HR's ability to ignite the spark of confidence within the workforce—and within leadership—is crucial for driving change. The outside/in perspective requires HR to be a beacon of trust, not just for employees but also for external stakeholders.

Practical example: Take a situation where an organization is facing criticism from the public over its diversity and inclusion practices. HR can ignite the spark by spearheading initiatives that address these concerns head-on, not just involving internal stakeholders but also engaging with the community and external partners. By taking the lead on transparency and accountability, HR builds trust internally and externally, enhancing the organization's reputation.

BRING CLARITY FROM THE CLOUDS

Dave's outside/in approach requires HR to provide clear, actionable insights based on how the organization is performing in real-time. HR professionals must be able to cut through complexity and bring clarity to both leadership and employees, helping the organization make informed decisions quickly.

Practical example: During the Covid-19 pandemic, many organizations were forced to adapt rapidly to remote work. HR's role in bringing clarity to this chaotic situation was critical. By establishing clear communication channels, providing updated policies on remote work, and ensuring employees had the tools they needed to stay productive, HR could keep the organization functioning smoothly in the midst of uncertainty.

FORWARD AND ADAPTIVE BEATS STATIC AND SLOW

Dave's emphasis on agility aligns perfectly with the value of being forward and adaptive. HR cannot afford to be static; it must adapt to the fast-paced changes in both the external market and internal organizational needs. This means staying ahead of trends in work-force dynamics, technology, and customer expectations.

Practical example: As artificial intelligence becomes more preva-lent in the workplace, HR leaders must proactively assess how AI will impact talent management. By developing training programs that prepare employees for AI-driven tasks and by adjusting hiring crite-ria to reflect new skills needed in the workforce, HR can ensure the organization remains competitive in an increasingly tech-driven world.

Building a Leadership Brand

One of the most compelling points from my conversation with Dave was the idea of creating a "leadership brand." Just as a company's product brand sets expectations for quality and experience, a leader-ship brand defines how leaders throughout the organization should behave and what results they should deliver. Leadership brand exists when leaders consistently demonstrate behaviors that align with both the organization's values and the expectations of its customers and shareholders.

According to Dave, there are six key steps to building a leadership brand:

1 **Create a need for leadership brand:** Before making investments in leadership development, the senior team must recognize its value. The goal is to help the company achieve better financial and customer outcomes through stronger leadership.

2 **Articulate a declaration of leadership:** This declaration sets clear standards for what leaders at all levels should know, do, and deliver. It combines leadership competencies with desired business results.

3 **Assess leaders against the brand standard:** With the standards set, HR can collect data—often through 360-degree assessments—to evaluate whether leaders are meeting the brand expectations.

4 **Invest in leaders:** Based on assessment data, HR can tailor leadership development programs to address specific gaps. This

could involve a mix of training, on-the-job experience, and mentorship.

5 **Measure the impact of leadership investments:** Leadership development must be tied to measurable business outcomes. By tracking metrics like employee engagement or customer satisfaction, HR can demonstrate the ROI of leadership investments.

6 **Publicize the leadership brand:** HR should ensure that the leadership brand is well-known both internally and externally, building confidence in the company's leadership for all stakeholders.

Evolving HR Metrics with Analytics

Another important aspect of our conversation was the role of analytics in HR. Dave outlined four stages of analytics evolution, each offering different insights and benefits:

- **Benchmarking:** This stage involves comparing the organization's performance with others in the industry. For HR, this might mean comparing employee engagement scores or retention rates with industry averages.

- **Best practice:** At this stage, HR identifies the best performers in the industry and analyzes what makes them successful. For example, HR might study how top companies in the field manage employee development and engagement.

- **Predictive analytics:** This involves using data to predict future trends or outcomes. For HR, this could mean using historical data to forecast turnover rates or employee performance.

- **Guidance:** The final stage of analytics involves providing actionable insights based on the data. Rather than just identifying trends, HR uses data to recommend specific actions that will drive business success.

By progressing through these stages, HR can move from being reactive to proactive, using data not just to report on what has happened but to shape what will happen next.

HR's Role in the Future of Work

As our conversation drew to a close, Dave shared his thoughts on how HR will continue to evolve in the coming decade. With advancements in technology and shifts in workforce dynamics, HR professionals will need to develop new skills to stay relevant. One of the key challenges, according to Dave, will be balancing the need for technological innovation with the human element of the workforce. While AI and automation will play a larger role in business operations, the ability to manage, develop, and engage people will remain critical.

In this future landscape, HR leaders must focus on four key agendas:

1 **Value to stakeholders:** Organizations only exist as long as they provide value to stakeholders, including customers, investors, and communities. HR must always consider how its actions impact these groups.

2 **An integrated solution:** HR needs to develop an integrated framework that addresses talent, organization, leadership, and the HR function itself. This holistic approach ensures that all aspects of human capability are aligned to drive business success.

3 **Evidence over stories:** While stories of success can be inspiring, they are not always reliable. HR must rely on evidence-based practices grounded in research and data to make decisions that have a lasting impact.

4 **Learning from the past:** As Dave pointed out, many of the timeless principles of HR remain relevant today. By learning from the past and applying those lessons to modern challenges, HR can continue to evolve without losing sight of its core values.

In conclusion, my conversation with Dave Ulrich reinforced the idea that HR has the power to drive real business success, but only if we embrace a forward-thinking, outside/in approach. By aligning HR practices with both internal goals and external realities, we can ensure that HR remains a strategic partner in shaping the future of work.

Beyond the Norm: When HR Challenges the Status Quo

Challenging the status quo is essential for HR to drive innovation and create a competitive advantage. Not simply to change things for the sake of change, but rather to ensure the future competitive success of your organization. In today's rapidly evolving business landscape, HR professionals must be bold, proactive, and willing to push boundaries to foster a culture of continuous improvement and transformation.

As senior HR professionals, our role is not just to manage processes but to lead change. By challenging traditional practices, we can unlock new opportunities for growth, enhance employee engagement, and position our organizations for long-term success. However, not every executive or employee will inherently want to change. It's tough rolling out a new payroll system, it's difficult transitioning to an unlimited PTO plan, and it's a struggle to set new pay bands as you try to reset salary expectations during trying economic times. But that is the role we play within our organizations, and it is essential that we embrace this as our power, not our problem. We move organizations forward! In this section, we will explore why challenging the status quo is crucial and how we can effectively do so.

Understanding the Need to Challenge the Status Quo

Challenging the status quo means questioning existing practices, policies, and assumptions to identify areas for improvement and innovation. It is about moving beyond 'the way things have always been done' to embrace new ideas and approaches. This mindset is crucial for staying competitive in a dynamic business environment.

You may have heard the story of why Redbox, a physical DVD rental kiosk company, failed to compete and scale at the same pace as Netflix, a digital streaming subscription service. If you haven't, it is the story of one company which believed its success was heavily dependent upon widespread adoption of DVD and Blu-ray players (Redbox), whereas the other believed its success was pivoting from physical DVDs and Blu-ray discs into the growing trend of streaming content on a subscription basis. The purpose of this book is to help provide context of why changing the status quo matters. The Netflix story is one of an industry startup challenging the status quo.

But what about the countless CHROs and HR Directors who navigated their organizations through the labor challenges of the Covid-19 pandemic? Those leaders were not 'just doing their job,' they were heroes we should look to when understanding why HR must meet the moment and respond in a way that helps our organizations thrive and maintain relevance.

EVALUATE THE CURRENT LANDSCAPE

Have you ever wondered why your phone goes through so many software and app upgrades? I can't go a week without some of my mainstay apps like LinkedIn and Instagram pushing out a refresh. What was wrong with the old version? Can't we just stick with the software that was initially loaded on our phones and face the new challenges of today with software from the past?

There are several reasons why that answer is no. Sometimes upgrades are for security reasons. A vulnerability was discovered, and a patch needed to be released to make the app safe. Other times the upgrades are for operational reasons. There's a feature that doesn't work the way it was intended, and enough users have alerted the software company to the issue. And lastly, there are times where apps upgrade for performance reasons. The company has determined that changing the user experience of the app or adding/removing features is the best way to secure an engaged mass of people who download, use, and tell the world about the app that they enjoy.

Why don't we look at HR operations in that same way? Many traditional HR practices, while once effective, may no longer meet the needs of your workforce or business environment. There could be security concerns, flaws in execution of HR standard operating procedures or reasons to challenge the status quo that have more to do with the world around us changing and our internal views must adapt. An example of a security concern would be the need to train staff on cybersecurity threats on a regular basis, since so much of our business these days is conducted online and on cloud services. One example of a flaw in execution would be that conventional performance management systems often focus on annual reviews, which can be ineffective in providing timely feedback and development. An example of external change would be the changing legal landscape with respect to access to women's reproductive health medical services and the need to develop healthcare strategies that align with your company values and employee medical needs. To thrive, we must continuously evaluate and evolve our practices.

KEY AREAS FOR CHALLENGING THE STATUS QUO

Talent Acquisition   Innovative approaches to recruiting and hiring can significantly enhance our ability to attract and retain top talent. For instance, leveraging AI and machine learning can streamline the recruitment process, reduce bias, and improve candidate matching. Companies have successfully implemented AI-driven recruitment platforms to enhance efficiency and candidate experience. In a white paper entitled "AI in the Modern Workplace" (UKG, 2024), we learn that McDonald's has adopted conversational AI in its recruiting practices, an effort that has shortened the application process in a high-turnover industry to hours rather than weeks.

Performance Management   Rethinking performance reviews and feedback mechanisms can lead to more effective employee development. Instead of relying solely on annual reviews, we can implement continuous performance management systems that provide ongoing feedback and support. Adobe, for example, replaced traditional performance reviews with 'Check-In' conversations, resulting in higher employee satisfaction and engagement (Adobe, 2024).

Employee Engagement   Creating new strategies to enhance employee engagement and satisfaction is vital. Introducing flexible work arrangements, wellness programs, and opportunities for professional growth can significantly impact employee morale and productivity. Google's focus on employee wellbeing, through initiatives like flexible working hours and wellness programs, has been instrumental in maintaining high engagement levels (Google, 2022).

Learning and Development "Modernizing training and development programs can ensure our workforce remains agile and skilled. Utilizing e-learning platforms, personalized learning paths, and interactive training methods can enhance learning outcomes. AT&T, for instance, invested heavily in reskilling its workforce through online courses and development programs, enabling employees to stay ahead of technological advancements" (Donovan and Benko, 2016).

Strategies for Successfully Challenging the Status Quo

BUILDING A BUSINESS CASE
Developing a compelling case for innovative changes is the first step. This involves presenting clear objectives, a thorough cost-benefit analysis, and a risk assessment. For example, when proposing a new talent acquisition strategy, we should highlight the expected improvements in hiring efficiency, quality of hire, and overall cost savings.

GAINING LEADERSHIP SUPPORT
Securing buy-in from executive leadership is crucial for driving change. This requires presenting the potential return on investment and aligning the proposed changes with organizational goals. For instance, presenting data on how continuous performance management can enhance productivity and align with the company's growth strategy can help gain leadership support.

PILOT PROGRAMS AND ITERATIVE IMPROVEMENTS
Testing new approaches through pilot programs allows us to gather feedback, make adjustments, and demonstrate the initiative's value before full-scale implementation. For example, launching a pilot program for a new employee engagement initiative can help identify potential challenges and refine the approach based on initial results.

Overcoming Resistance

IDENTIFYING AND ADDRESSING CONCERNS

Understanding and addressing resistance from stakeholders is essential. This involves engaging employees and managers in the design and implementation of new practices to ensure their concerns are heard and addressed. For instance, conducting focus groups and feedback sessions can provide valuable insights into potential resistance points and ways to mitigate them.

COMMUNICATION AND EDUCATION

Communicating the benefits of change and educating stakeholders about new initiatives can help ease the transition. This includes hosting workshops, training sessions, and providing ongoing support to ensure everyone is on board. For example, rolling out a comprehensive communication plan that outlines the benefits of a new performance management system can help gain employee acceptance and support.

In summary, challenging the status quo is vital for driving innovation and staying competitive. Key areas for innovation include talent acquisition, performance management, employee engagement, and learning and development. By building a strong business case, gaining leadership support, testing new approaches, and addressing resistance, we can successfully implement innovative HR practices.

> As HR professionals, we must embrace the mindset of continuous improvement and be willing to challenge traditional practices. By doing so, we can lead our organizations to new heights of success and create a more dynamic, engaged, and productive workforce.

"By challenging the status quo, HR can lead the way in driving innovation and creating a competitive edge for the organization. Let's commit to pushing boundaries and transforming our HR practices for a brighter future."—Joey Price

CASE STUDY EXERCISE

The Case for Consistency

You are the HR director at a midsize luxury women's clothing e-commerce company, LuxeWear US. Recently, you have noticed a series of complaints from the marketing team about inconsistent performance feedback following repeated turnover of their manager. The team has experienced three different managers in the past year, leading to a lack of clear performance expectations and feedback consistency. As a result, employee morale and productivity have declined, and there is growing dissatisfaction within the team.

To address this issue, you need to devise a strategy to establish a consistent performance feedback process. Additionally, you are considering implementing performance management software to streamline and standardize feedback across the organization.

Please note: This case study is entirely fictitious. Any relationship to a real-world organization or person is entirely coincidental.

Task

Develop a strategy to recommend a process for establishing clear and consistent performance feedback. Your strategy should include the steps for selecting and implementing a performance management software. Be sure to consider the specific needs and challenges of the marketing team and how your recommendations can improve overall employee satisfaction and performance. Ideally, your recommendations should also be able to apply to other departments within your team so that there is consistency in performance feedback for everyone.

Supporting Questions

- What are the key issues resulting from the inconsistent feedback experienced by the marketing team?
- What are the essential components of an effective performance feedback process?
- What features should you look for in performance management software to support your feedback process?
- What steps will you take to implement the new performance feedback process and software?

- How will you measure the success of the new performance feedback process and software implementation?

HR Success Checklist: Daily, Weekly, Monthly, Quarterly, and Annual Activities

Create a detailed plan outlining your strategy for establishing a consistent performance feedback process and implementing performance management software. Your plan should include a timeline, key milestones, and metrics for success. Be prepared to present your recommendations to the executive team and address any questions or concerns they may have.

Consistency is key to success in any field, and HR is no exception. Implementing a structured HR success checklist ensures that we stay focused, organized, and aligned with our strategic goals. Below is a collection of daily, weekly, monthly, quarterly, and annual activities that can drive continuous improvement and success in our HR practices.

As senior HR professionals, our responsibilities are vast and varied. A well-defined checklist helps us manage our tasks efficiently and effectively, ensuring that we consistently deliver value to our organizations. Let's dive into the specific actions we can take on a daily, weekly, monthly, quarterly, and annual basis to achieve HR success.

Daily Activities

MONITOR KEY METRICS
Every day, it's crucial to monitor key HR metrics such as employee engagement, turnover, and performance. This helps us stay informed about the current state of our workforce and identify any emerging issues early. Utilizing HR software and dashboards allows us to track these metrics in real-time. For instance, checking daily attendance

reports can highlight patterns of absenteeism that may require further investigation.

EMPLOYEE FEEDBACK

Collecting and responding to employee feedback on a daily basis fosters a culture of open communication and continuous improvement. Implementing daily check-ins and feedback systems, such as quick surveys or suggestion boxes, ensures that employees feel heard and valued. For example, a simple daily pulse survey can provide insights into employee morale and satisfaction, allowing us to address concerns promptly. And do not underestimate the power of responding to staff emails in a timely fashion. This is an important way to continue to earn a trusted reputation.

Weekly Activities

TEAM MEETINGS

Holding weekly HR team meetings is essential for discussing progress, addressing concerns, and reviewing key metrics. These meetings foster open communication, collaboration, and alignment within the HR team. During these sessions, we can review ongoing projects, share updates, and brainstorm solutions to any challenges we face. For example, a weekly meeting can be used to discuss the progress of a new recruitment campaign and adjust strategies as needed.

PERFORMANCE REVIEWS

Conducting weekly performance reviews and check-ins with employees helps provide ongoing support and address any challenges they may be facing. Regular check-ins ensure that employees receive timely feedback and recognition, which can boost their motivation and performance. For instance, a brief weekly check-in can help managers and employees discuss short-term goals, progress, and any obstacles that need to be addressed. For more helpful advice on frequent check-ins, refer to Adobe's "Check-In" model (Adobe, 2024).

Monthly Activities

ENGAGEMENT SURVEYS

Conducting monthly engagement surveys allows us to gather feedback and identify areas for improvement. Analyzing the results helps us understand trends and make necessary adjustments to enhance employee engagement. Monthly surveys can be more comprehensive than daily pulse checks, providing deeper insights into employee satisfaction and areas for development. For example, a monthly survey might explore themes like work–life, career development opportunities, and workplace culture.

TRAINING AND DEVELOPMENT

Scheduling monthly training sessions or workshops on HR best practices and other relevant topics supports continuous learning and professional development. Encouraging participation in these activities helps HR professionals stay updated with the latest trends and improve their skills. For instance, a monthly workshop on diversity and inclusion can equip HR staff with the knowledge and tools needed to foster an inclusive workplace.

Quarterly Activities

COMPREHENSIVE REVIEWS

Conducting quarterly comprehensive reviews of all HR initiatives and their impact provides an opportunity to evaluate our progress and make strategic adjustments. These reviews should include a thorough analysis of key performance indicators (KPIs) and feedback from stakeholders. For example, a quarterly review might assess the effectiveness of a new onboarding program, incorporating feedback from new hires and managers to refine the process.

STRATEGIC PLANNING

Developing a strategic plan for the next quarter helps ensure that HR initiatives are aligned with business goals. This involves setting clear objectives, identifying priorities, and allocating resources effectively. Engaging stakeholders in the planning process ensures that the HR strategy supports the overall organizational strategy. For instance, a quarterly planning session might focus on workforce planning, identifying key talent needs for upcoming projects and initiatives.

Annual Activities

ANNUAL REPORT

Preparing an annual report summarizing HR contributions, key metrics, and impact on organizational success highlights the value of HR to the organization. This report should be presented to leadership and stakeholders, showcasing achievements and identifying areas for future focus. For example, the annual report might include data on employee retention, diversity initiatives, and the outcomes of leadership development programs.

STRATEGIC REVIEW

Conducting an annual strategic review assesses the effectiveness of HR initiatives over the past year and plans for the coming year. This review should involve a comprehensive evaluation of HR's impact on the organization and identify opportunities for improvement. Engaging key stakeholders in this process ensures that HR's strategic direction aligns with the broader business goals. For instance, the annual strategic review might set new targets for employee engagement and outline initiatives to enhance organizational culture.

I encourage you to adopt and customize this checklist to fit your organization's needs. By consistently following these actions, you can demonstrate HR's impact, drive continuous improvement, and support your organization's success.

Reflecting on HR's Role in Business Growth

As HR professionals, we must consistently ask ourselves how well our strategies align with our organization's overarching business goals. It's not enough to simply manage talent or administer benefits. HR should be a strategic partner, driving the company's mission forward. This alignment is crucial, and it starts by understanding where the business is headed and ensuring that every HR initiative, whether it's hiring, talent development, or employee engagement, is directly contributing to those goals.

For example, if the company's goal is expansion into new markets, we need to assess whether we're hiring the right talent, building leadership pipelines, and creating a culture that supports growth. This is where the HR value of owning your expertise comes into play. It's about using your knowledge of people and organizational dynamics to craft strategies that not only support the company but propel it toward its objectives.

Talent management is another critical area. How are we ensuring that our workforce is not just capable but continually evolving? Forward and adaptive beats static and slow—we must develop talent management practices that foster growth, agility, and resilience. It's about more than filling positions; it's about building a team that can weather change and lead the business through transformation. Implementing structured career development programs, leadership training, and mentorship initiatives are just some ways to ensure our talent is equipped to support business growth.

When it comes to employee engagement, we have to ask: How engaged are our people with their work? Engagement isn't a "nice to have"—it's a critical driver of productivity and innovation. Igniting the spark is essential here. We need to create environments where employees feel valued, motivated, and aligned with the company's mission. This involves actively listening to employees, offering opportunities for professional growth, and recognizing their contributions in meaningful ways. Engagement doesn't happen in a vacuum; it's nurtured through intentional HR practices.

Measuring the success of our HR initiatives is another area where we need to be diligent. What metrics are we using, and how do they inform our strategies? This ties back to the value of bringing clarity from the clouds. Clear, measurable outcomes help us assess whether our efforts are making an impact. Are we using data to not only track engagement and performance but also predict future trends? KPIs, like employee retention, productivity rates, and feedback scores, are essential, but we should also be exploring predictive analytics that allow us to anticipate workforce needs and trends. Data-driven decision-making is non-negotiable in today's fast-paced environment.

To remain at the forefront of HR leadership, we must also be committed to continuous learning. The business world—and the HR function within it—evolves constantly. New technologies, employee expectations, and legal requirements are shifting, and it's our responsibility to stay ahead of these changes. Whether through formal education, professional networks, or industry conferences, we need to embrace learning as an ongoing process, not just an occasional activity. HR leaders who stay informed bring innovation and relevance to their organizations.

Lastly, we must constantly give feedback and embrace candor. HR can't afford to not be truth tellers in our organizations. Be part coach, part cheerleader—we should be regularly providing feedback to employees, managers, and stakeholders to improve our processes. The most successful HR teams are those that are willing to adapt, refine, and grow based on real-time insights. Regular feedback loops ensure that we're continuously improving and adjusting to the changing needs of the business.

In summary, HR's role in business growth is profound. By aligning strategies with business goals, managing and developing talent effectively, driving employee engagement, and staying committed to continuous improvement, we can ensure that HR is not just a support function but a true driver of organizational success. The power of HR lies in its ability to influence every aspect of the business, and by embodying these values, we create lasting impact.

Conclusion

As you reflect on the insights shared in this chapter, I want you to remember the impact HR can have when it is fully leveraged. The challenges we face as HR professionals are often complex, but with those challenges come opportunities to truly lead. We are more than administrative support. We are catalysts for change, influencers in the boardroom, and champions of the employee experience. Through your efforts, you have the ability to drive not only organizational success but also positive, lasting change in the lives of the people who make up your company.

By aligning HR strategies with business objectives, managing talent with foresight, and fostering a culture of engagement, you are shaping the future of work. Whether you're introducing new processes, navigating performance management systems, or leading the charge in employee engagement, your work is critical to the long-term health and success of your organization.

HR has the power to redefine business outcomes, and you are the person at the helm. You are the key to unlocking potential—not just for the company but for every individual within it. Take pride in that role, and know that every small step you take toward improvement is a giant leap toward creating a stronger, more resilient organization.

References

Adobe (2024) Adobe Check-in, www.adobe.com/check-in.html (archived at https://perma.cc/E4FE-H4UN)

Google (2022) Action #4: Flexibility—Google Diversity Annual Report. about.google/belonging/diversity-annual-report/2022/flexibility/ (archived at https://perma.cc/F8VW-5GP4)

Harter, J (2024) In New Workplace, U.S. Employee Engagement Stagnates, Gallup.com, www.gallup.com/workplace/608675/new-workplace-employee-engagement-stagnates.aspx (archived at https://perma.cc/4XNT-RGZQ)

UKG (2024) AI in the Modern Workplace, ukg.com, www.ukg.com/resources/white-paper/ai-modern-workplace (archived at https://perma.cc/HF4Z-W2UK)

2

Demonstrating Value to the Organization

Introduction

In this chapter, I want to talk in greater detail about a critical aspect of our work as HR professionals: aligning our HR value proposition with our organization's business objectives. In a world where the business environment is constantly evolving, ensuring that HR's goals are in sync with the broader business strategy is not just important—it's essential for driving our professional and organizational success.

In the ever-evolving world of HR, delivering real business value can transform careers and organizations. This fictional story of Alex Ramirez illustrates the journey from being a people-focused HR generalist to a strategic HR leader who aligns employee initiatives with business goals, driving both personal growth and company success.

Story of Impact: HR's Value Realized

In the heart of Oklahoma City, an HR generalist named Alex Ramirez found himself at a crucial juncture in his career. Working at Nexus Innovations, a Fortune 500 company renowned for its innovative solutions, Alex was known for his empathetic approach and unwavering support for the employees. However, as the company grew, so did the demands on its HR team.

One morning, Alex walked into the office of the Chief People Officer. He had been anticipating this meeting, hoping it would bring good news about the promotion he had been eyeing for months.

"Alex, you are a cornerstone of our team," the CPO began, her expression earnest. "Your dedication to our people is unparalleled, but to move up, you need to demonstrate more business acumen. We need HR leaders who can align our people strategy with our business goals."

Alex left the office with a heavy heart. He had always prided himself on leading from the heart, but now he needed to learn how to deliver tangible business value. Unsure of where to start, he reached out to me, hoping for guidance.

Over a video call, Alex laid out his predicament. I listened intently and then offered a roadmap. "Alex, every successful HR leader needs to understand and leverage core business metrics. This is what will set you apart."

I provided Alex with a list of key metrics to master: employee turnover rates, cost per hire, employee engagement scores, and the impact of training programs on productivity. I also suggested he enroll in a course on business analytics at the local university to deepen his understanding.

Motivated and determined, Alex followed the advice. He juggled his work and studies, applying what he learned in real-time at Nexus Innovations. He began presenting data-driven insights during team meetings, proposing strategies that not only improved employee satisfaction but also contributed to the company's bottom line.

Six months later, Alex found himself once again in the CPO's office. This time, the atmosphere was different. She smiled warmly, "Alex, your transformation has been remarkable. Your ability to link our HR initiatives with business outcomes has not gone unnoticed. I am pleased to inform you that you have been promoted to HR Manager."

As Alex walked out of the office, he felt a surge of pride and accomplishment. He had not only advanced in his career, but had also grown as a leader. His journey underscored a vital lesson: leading from the heart is important, but delivering business value is what drives an organization forward.

At the next all-hands meeting, Alex shared his story with his colleagues. "HR is not just about people," he said, "it's about understanding how our people contribute to the bigger picture. When we bridge the gap between empathy and business acumen, we truly realize our value."

His words resonated deeply, inspiring many in the room to think about their roles in a new light. Alex's journey, much like the one you are about to explore in this book, highlighted the transformative power of HR in driving organizational success.

HR Value Proposition: Aligning with Business Objectives

For senior HR professionals, understanding and communicating the value we bring to the organization is key. By aligning our initiatives with business objectives, we can demonstrate our strategic importance, drive impactful results, and gain the support and trust of leadership. Let's explore how we can achieve this alignment and effectively communicate our HR value proposition.

Understanding the HR Value Proposition

The HR value proposition is the unique value that HR delivers to an organization. It encompasses all the ways in which HR contributes to achieving business goals, from attracting and retaining top talent to fostering a positive organizational culture and driving performance improvements. Our role is to ensure that these contributions are aligned with the strategic objectives of the business.

Now would be a good time to express a point of clarification that tends to cause rifts between HR and leadership. We should be absolutely clear that HR initiatives serve to support the business objectives—not the other way around. Think about the Marketing department in your organization. Does it not exist to advance the overall business mission of increased customer retention, greater product or service awareness, and more sales? Or what about your Accounting department? The purpose of the Accounting department is to properly forecast, account for, and manage the financial aspects of the business. So, if all other department initiatives serve the overall organization, why wouldn't we expect HR to do so as well?

I believe that this is due, in part, to a failure to understand that HR's mission is truly to create the best environment for human resources to thrive and produce meaningful returns for their efforts. We do not operate primarily for the joy and comfort of staff, but rather as the department that must successfully manage the tension that exists between executive demands for performance and staff demands for meeting their needs. Next, we must unpack the importance of alignment.

Why is this alignment so crucial? First of all, it ensures that our efforts are focused on areas that matter most to the business. Second of all, it helps us secure the resources and support we need to be effective. Lastly, it allows us to measure and demonstrate the impact of our initiatives in terms that are meaningful to the organization. The power of an HR practitioner's influence and outcomes rests in our ability to advance the organization's mission while everyone is having as good a time as possible.

Key Components of Aligning HR with Business Objectives

BUSINESS UNDERSTANDING

To align HR with business objectives, we must first have a deep understanding of the business itself. This means knowing the company's mission, vision, and strategic goals. We need to understand the market dynamics, competitive landscape, and key challenges the organization faces. By staying informed about these factors, we can ensure that our HR strategies are relevant and impactful.

In order to do this, you must ensure you are doing all that you can to immerse yourself into the world of your industry. Start by meeting with leaders in other functions of the business to get a sense for their priorities, motivations, and goals. Ask them what has prepared them to lead the department and where they would like for it to go. Ask them to give their perspective of the company's place in the competitive landscape and any strengths, weaknesses, opportunities, and threats from their perspective. You will be fascinated when you receive various takes on that question!

It's also important to be sure you do not limit yourself to knowledge of your industry within the silo of what fellow staff members tell you. Take time to study competitor websites, read industry journals and publications, join industry associations, and volunteer for leadership positions. The more you know about your industry—and your organization's place within it—the more you can make strategic recommendations that are informed by business knowledge, not just HR best practices.

INTEGRATED HR STRATEGIES

Developing integrated HR strategies that support and drive business goals is essential. For example, if one of the company's strategic goals is to expand into new markets, our HR strategy should focus on building the capabilities required for this expansion. This could involve identifying skill gaps, developing targeted recruitment campaigns, and implementing training programs to prepare employees for new roles.

PERFORMANCE METRICS

Establishing performance metrics that align HR activities with business outcomes is critical. These metrics should be specific, measurable, and tied directly to business objectives. For instance, if the organization aims to improve customer satisfaction, HR can contribute by enhancing employee engagement and training programs, as there is a direct link between engaged employees and satisfied customers. By tracking metrics like employee engagement scores and customer feedback, we can demonstrate how HR initiatives contribute to achieving business goals.

COLLABORATIVE PLANNING

Involving HR in the strategic planning process ensures alignment and integration. This means having a seat at the table during executive strategy sessions and planning meetings. By participating in these discussions, we can align our initiatives with the overall business strategy and ensure that HR is seen as a strategic partner rather than a support function. Collaboration with other departments is also crucial to understand their needs and align our HR strategies accordingly.

Strategies for Achieving Alignment

REGULAR COMMUNICATION

Maintaining regular communication between HR and other internal business leaders is key to ensuring ongoing alignment. This can be achieved through regular updates, strategy meetings, and progress reports. By keeping the lines of communication open, we can stay aligned with the business's changing needs and priorities. Regularly sharing updates on HR initiatives and their impact also helps build trust and demonstrate the value of our contributions. I also would recommend joining department meetings from time to time. After all, how can you truly grasp department priorities and team dynamics if you only manage HR from your comfort zone?

FLEXIBLE HR PRACTICES

Developing adaptable HR practices that can evolve with the business needs is essential. This means being agile and responsive to changes in the business environment. For example, if the organization is going through a digital transformation, HR should be ready to support this transition by developing digital skills training programs and implementing change management strategies. By staying flexible, we can ensure that our HR practices remain relevant and effective. Your ability to master when to be flexible and when to be firm for the good of alignment will help your fellow executive peers appreciate the art and science of human resources management and development.

DATA-DRIVEN DECISION-MAKING

Leveraging data and analytics to inform HR decisions and demonstrate impact is increasingly important. By using data to identify trends, measure outcomes, and make informed decisions, we can ensure that our initiatives are aligned with business objectives and deliver tangible results. For example, using predictive analytics to identify potential turnover risks allows us to take proactive measures to retain key talent. By presenting data-driven insights to leadership, we can make a compelling case for our strategies and demonstrate their value.

In summary, aligning our HR value proposition with business objectives involves understanding the business, developing integrated HR strategies, establishing performance metrics, and participating in collaborative planning. By maintaining regular communication, developing flexible HR practices, and leveraging data-driven decision-making, we can ensure that our initiatives are aligned with the strategic goals of the organization.

> As HR professionals, it's our responsibility to align our efforts with the broader business strategy. By doing so, we can drive impactful results, demonstrate our strategic importance, and contribute to the overall success of our organizations.

Mentor's Corner: Modern Organizational Challenges Only HR Can Solve

Let's talk about how HR leaders can amplify their value to the organization in a more meaningful way than just responding to the day-to-day. Demonstrating value isn't about simply doing what's required—it's about seizing opportunities that drive both workforce excellence and business growth. This means stepping beyond reactive measures and implementing forward-thinking strategies that establish HR as a key player in shaping the future of the business.

As the workforce has evolved over the past decade, there are challenges that I believe HR is uniquely positioned to help organizations overcome. Using our five HR values as a guide, let's discuss these unique opportunities.

Shaping AI as a Strategic Partner in Workforce Evolution

The conversation around artificial intelligence in the workplace is no longer about "if" but "how" to integrate it. As an HR leader, your role isn't to wait for someone else to define what AI means for your organization—you will bring significant value to the organization if you are at the forefront, shaping how this technology can be leveraged to make work more meaningful, efficient, and productive. As I reference in my TEDx talk entitled "Talent & Tech: Embracing Collaboration with AI for Workplace Success" (Price, 2023), AI shouldn't be something that replaces the human element, but rather a tool that enhances it. As HR, you know where the administrative bottlenecks lie, where processes can be streamlined, and where teams need support. AI can do the heavy lifting on repetitive tasks, and it's your opportunity to align AI capabilities with your company's human needs.

Take the lead by advocating for AI's thoughtful integration—whether that's automating recruitment processes, using AI to handle data-heavy tasks like payroll, or enhancing employee engagement through predictive analytics. AI is here to help you amplify the human in human resources. When you adopt and advocate for these technologies, you demonstrate HR's ability to directly impact the organization's efficiency and innovation. It also positions you as a forward-thinking strategist, not just a gatekeeper.

Mental Health as a Core Business Strategy

Moving the needle on employee mental health has become more than just an HR initiative—it's a business imperative. Senior leadership may see mental health as a wellness benefit, but you can drive this concept further. Your seat in the organization allows you to connect the dots between mental health and business outcomes. When employees feel supported mentally, they are not only more engaged but also more loyal, more productive, and less likely to burn out. This is a clear bottom-line issue.

As an HR leader, it's essential to own your expertise and be the internal advocate for mental health initiatives that go beyond surface-level solutions. You should be making the case that mental health drives key performance indicators like employee engagement, retention, and overall productivity. Build these arguments with real data—gather feedback through employee surveys, track absenteeism related to stress, and create ROI models that demonstrate the financial benefits of investing in comprehensive mental health support.

Moreover, to truly ignite the spark and show your influence, HR should also be involved in shaping the organizational culture to be one where mental health is openly discussed and supported. It's about fostering an environment where mental wellbeing is treated as an ongoing priority, not a one-off program. By pushing the conversation beyond wellness days to integrated mental health solutions, you solidify HR's strategic role in maintaining a productive, engaged workforce. This is not just a "nice-to-have" approach to wellbeing. According to the Surgeon General of the United States (Office of the U.S. Surgeon General and H. Murthy, n.d.) toxic workplace culture is a global health issue, and he's published a 48-page framework to combat its effects.

Redefining Flexibility: The Future of Work

The discussion around flexible work arrangements, like the four-day workweek, isn't just a passing trend. As HR leaders, it's critical to explore these concepts as potential long-term solutions that align employee wellbeing with business performance. Flexibility in work schedules, remote work policies, and creative working models isn't just about retention—it's about productivity and innovation.

By positioning HR at the helm of this change, you become a key driver in how your company evolves. But how can you ensure that these flexible models truly work? HR should lead pilot programs that test flexible work arrangements, collecting both quantitative and qualitative feedback. Evaluate performance, employee satisfaction, and even client feedback to refine these models to work best for your organization.

HR's role isn't just to implement the changes leadership wants to see—it's to provide leadership with the insights and data that support flexible work models as a strategic move that boosts both morale and output. By bringing clarity from the clouds, you translate vague concepts of "work–life balance" into actionable frameworks that directly contribute to the business's success.

Managing a Multigenerational Workforce: Leading with Inclusion

The challenge of a multigenerational workforce often feels like balancing opposing needs and priorities. Older generations may favor traditional work structures, while younger employees might prioritize purpose and flexibility. Rather than seeing this diversity as a problem to solve, view it as an opportunity to strengthen the organization.

To demonstrate value here, you should focus on building bridges between these different generational cohorts. This means developing mentorship programs that foster cross-generational learning, offering leadership development that speaks to each group's unique needs, and creating opportunities for every generation to see their contributions as part of the larger organizational mission.

By fostering these initiatives, HR proves itself as the coach and cheerleader for the organization, encouraging collaboration, knowledge transfer, and mutual respect among employees. Not only does this improve workplace harmony, it also creates a more dynamic and innovative workforce, where diverse perspectives are valued.

Leveraging the Five HR Values to Drive Impact

Now let's take a deeper dive into how the five HR values align with driving value to your organization.

OWN YOUR EXPERTISE

Owning your expertise means confidently stepping into strategic discussions with data-driven insights and a clear understanding of how HR initiatives support business objectives. You're not just the administrator—you're the strategist who aligns people with purpose. Whether it's through AI, mental health initiatives, or workforce planning, take charge of your knowledge and ensure that your leadership understands how HR is shaping the future of the organization.

BE PART COACH, PART CHEERLEADER

HR's role isn't just about enforcing policies—it's about fostering a culture where people feel empowered and supported. You are the coach that guides the organization through change and the cheerleader that motivates the team to reach higher. By building programs that encourage growth, leadership, and employee wellbeing, you show the company that HR's influence goes beyond transactional tasks.

IGNITE THE SPARK

The real value HR brings to the table is the ability to create a sense of engagement and purpose among employees. When HR drives initiatives that excite, motivate, and inspire the workforce, it boosts productivity and loyalty. Your role is to be the ignition point for innovation, inclusion, and passion within the workplace.

BRING CLARITY FROM THE CLOUDS

One of HR's greatest contributions is its ability to take complex challenges—whether it's integrating new technology, navigating cultural shifts, or managing organizational change—and break them down into clear, actionable steps. Your value is in making the intangible tangible, translating vision into action, and ensuring both employees and leadership have the roadmap they need to succeed.

FORWARD AND ADAPTIVE BEATS STATIC AND SLOW

In a rapidly evolving workplace, HR can't afford to be reactive. You need to be proactive, always looking ahead to the next trend, challenge, or opportunity. Whether that's testing flexible work models or preparing the organization for technological disruption, HR's value is in its ability to stay ahead of the curve and lead the company through change with confidence and agility.

Conclusion: Building HR's Strategic Legacy

To demonstrate value to the organization, HR leaders must move beyond the basics of employee management and actively shape the company's future. By applying these five core values—Own Your Expertise; Be Part Coach, Part Cheerleader; Ignite the Spark; Bring Clarity From the Clouds; and Forward and Adaptive Beats Static and Slow—HR can transform from a supportive function into a critical driver of business success.

Remember, HR isn't just there to solve problems—it's there to create opportunities. By leading with innovation, empathy, and strategy, you show that HR is a key player in driving sustainable growth, employee satisfaction, and organizational resilience. It's about positioning HR as the backbone of the business, not just its heart.

Exceptional Circumstances: When HR's Value Is Underestimated

If you've been working in HR for any number of years, you'll know there is one challenge that we all have experienced at one point or another. That's the challenge of HR's value being underestimated. Despite our significant contributions to organizational success, there are times when HR's impact is overlooked or undervalued. Understanding why this happens and how we can address it is crucial for enhancing our strategic influence and demonstrating our true worth.

As senior HR professionals, overcoming the challenge of being underestimated requires strategic action and a clear demonstration of our value. By understanding the factors that lead to this underestimation and implementing effective strategies to counteract it, we can ensure that HR is recognized as a critical driver of business success.

Understanding the Underestimation of HR's Value

COMMON MISCONCEPTIONS

There are several common misconceptions about HR that can lead to the underestimation of its value. These include the belief that HR is merely an administrative function, that our contributions are intangible and difficult to measure, and that HR's role is secondary to core business operations. These misconceptions can result in a lack of appreciation for the strategic impact that HR can have and this is not just a misconception we face at the senior leadership level, it permeates all throughout the organization.

In 2021, Forbes senior contributor Edward Segal published an article entitled 'Why Employees Don't Trust HR Staff—And What Can Be Done About It' (Segal, 2021) that shared the current state of HR vs. employee relations in the United States. The article shared the following statistics from a survey conducted by HR Software company Zenefits:

> "38% of employee respondents feel HR does not equally enforce company policies for all employees, with 18% of that group believing managers get special treatment." (Segal, 2021)
>
> "71% of HR employees in the survey stated that less than 30% of complaints they received in the last 2 years resulted in any disciplinary action." (Segal, 2021)

IMPACT OF UNDERESTIMATION

When HR's value is underestimated, it can lead to several negative consequences. These include insufficient resources and support for HR initiatives, reduced influence in strategic decision-making, and a lack of engagement from HR professionals who feel their contributions are undervalued. Ultimately, this can hinder our ability to drive meaningful change and support organizational goals.

Factors Leading to Underestimation

LACK OF QUANTIFIABLE METRICS

One major factor is the difficulty in quantifying HR's impact. While other departments can easily measure their contributions through financial metrics, HR's value often lies in areas like employee engagement, culture, and development, which are harder to quantify. This can make it challenging to demonstrate our impact in concrete terms.

I would encourage you to press through the underestimation and draw conclusions on the financial impact that HR operations have on the business. The more you can tie a dollar value to your initiatives, the more influence you will be able to attribute to HR's impact on company performance. If you need help with this, ask your HR colleague network for advice and meet with your CFO to define helpful financial models that reflect HR's expense or revenue added to the business.

STEREOTYPES AND BIASES

Stereotypes and biases about HR roles also contribute to underestimation. HR is sometimes viewed as a "soft" function that deals primarily with people issues and lacks the analytical rigor of other departments. This perception can prevent HR from being seen as a strategic partner.

We also wrestle with negative stereotypes in the media. A 2017 SHRM article entitled *Popular TV and Films Love to Hate HR* (Wilkie, 2017) lists the following movies and shows where HR is either the bad person or the brunt of jokes:

- *Up in the Air*
- *The Office* (US and UK)
- *The Drew Carey Show*

And you can probably think of others.

HISTORICAL ROLE OF HR

Historically, HR has been seen as an administrative function focused on compliance and paperwork. While the role of HR has evolved significantly, these outdated perceptions can still persist, leading to an underestimation of our strategic contributions.

This is exacerbated by working for CEOs and CFOs who fail to grasp the evolved role HR should play in today's business. Nowadays, my rule of thumb is to look at an organizational chart to see where the senior-most HR professional exists in the business. If the senior-most HR professional reports to Finance, then I believe the organization has stifled HR's potential impact on the business. If you are interviewing for a new role at an organization, ask for this information, it will give you the insight into the type of organization you are stepping into and their perspective about the value you bring.

Strategies to Overcome Underestimation

QUANTIFYING HR'S IMPACT

To address the challenge of quantifying our impact, we need to develop and track metrics that clearly demonstrate the value of HR initiatives. This includes measuring employee engagement, retention rates, productivity improvements, and the ROI of training and development programs. For example, linking employee engagement scores to customer satisfaction and financial performance can highlight the direct impact of HR on business outcomes.

BUILDING STRATEGIC PARTNERSHIPS

Building strong partnerships with other departments and positioning ourselves as strategic partners is essential. By collaborating with leaders across the organization and aligning our initiatives with business goals, we can demonstrate our strategic value. For instance, working closely with the Finance department to develop a business case for a new HR technology investment can help secure buy-in and resources. Similarly, working closely with the Marketing department to curate an effective employer brand will help improve quality of hire and retention because you are clearly conveying the employee experience to candidates who want to work for an organization that operates like yours.

COMMUNICATING VALUE EFFECTIVELY

Effective communication is key to overcoming underestimation. We need to clearly articulate the value of HR initiatives in terms that resonate with leadership. This includes using data and storytelling to highlight successes and making a compelling case for the strategic importance of HR. Regularly presenting updates and reports to the executive team can help keep HR's contributions top of mind.

INNOVATING AND ADAPTING

Innovation is another powerful way to demonstrate HR's value. By staying ahead of trends and continuously improving our practices, we can show that HR is a dynamic and forward-thinking function. Implementing cutting-edge technologies, adopting new talent management strategies, and fostering a culture of continuous improvement are all ways to highlight our innovative capabilities.

The only caveat I would add to this is that understanding your organizational culture is important here. Sometimes it is more important to prioritize efficiency of current methods than to introduce new methods that will force your organization to adapt to change at a pace that it is not ready to move at. This doesn't contradict the advice, but rather is a reminder that understanding your business is the most important aspect for determining the right value to bring to it.

ADVOCATING FOR HR

As HR leaders, we must also advocate for the importance of our function. This means championing HR at every opportunity, whether in strategic meetings, company-wide communications, or external forums. By being vocal advocates for HR, we can help shift perceptions and elevate the importance of our role. Take it one step further and find ways for your staff to advocate on your behalf. When you create wins for individual employees or other departments, ask for their testimonial so that it can be reported in future all-staff meetings or on your company intranet.

In summary, the underestimation of HR's value is a challenge that many of us face, but it is not insurmountable. By quantifying our impact, building strategic partnerships, communicating effectively, innovating, and advocating for HR, we can overcome this challenge and ensure that our contributions are recognized and valued.

I encourage you to take proactive steps to demonstrate and communicate the value of HR in your organization. By doing so, we can enhance our strategic influence, secure the resources we need, and drive greater success for our businesses.

CASE STUDY EXERCISE

Hire, Fire or Train?

You are the HR Director at large pharmaceuticals company, Gynysys, Inc. Despite positive results from FDA trials for your latest vaccine, the company has been facing declining sales performance over the past year. Senior leadership is seeking solutions to reverse this trend, and two primary options are being considered:

1 implementing comprehensive sales training programs to upskill the existing sales team

2 hiring a new experienced sales leader to drive sales performance and strategy

As the HR Director, you need to decide which option will provide the best return on investment and contribute most effectively to improving the company's sales performance. Your decision must be data-driven, and you will need to consider various metrics to support your choice.

Please note: This case study is entirely fictitious. Any relationship to a real-world organization or person is entirely coincidental.

Task

Develop a strategy to recommend either implementing sales training programs or hiring a new sales leader. Your strategy should include the key metrics to consider before making the decision and a plan to track the success or failure of the chosen option.

Supporting Questions

- What are the primary issues contributing to the declining sales performance at Gynysys, Inc.?
- How can HR play a role in addressing these issues?
- What are the potential benefits of implementing sales training programs for the existing team?
- What are the potential benefits of hiring a new experienced sales leader?
- What are the potential drawbacks of each option?

HR Value Checklist: Tracking and Reporting Value

Create a detailed plan outlining your recommendation for either implementing sales training programs or hiring a new sales leader. Your plan should include an analysis of key metrics, an implementation timeline, and a strategy for tracking success or failure. Be prepared to present your recommendation to the executive team and address any questions or concerns they may have. Since this is simply an exercise, you may assume and create data and metrics that support your position.

Tracking and reporting the value we bring to our organizations is an aspect of senior HR leadership that we must always be willing to incorporate into our schedule. In an increasingly data-driven world, demonstrating our impact through clear, measurable metrics is powerfully essential for securing support and driving strategic initiatives.

As senior HR leaders, our ability to track and report our contributions effectively not only validates our efforts but also strengthens our position as strategic partners within the organization. By implementing a comprehensive HR value checklist, we can ensure that our initiatives are aligned with business goals and that we can clearly communicate our successes to stakeholders.

Daily Activities

MONITOR KEY METRICS

Track daily attendance, productivity, and immediate issues using HR software.

Example: Review daily attendance reports to identify patterns of absenteeism. Tracking this data can help inform the need for temporary staff, staff augmentation, or employee assistance with time-off policies, disability insurance offerings, and leave programs.

EMPLOYEE FEEDBACK

Collect and respond to daily employee feedback through check-ins or quick surveys.

Example: Use daily pulse surveys to gauge employee morale and address concerns promptly. Take things one step further by drawing correlations to periods of high morale and higher-than-average profitability.

Weekly Activities

TEAM MEETINGS

Hold weekly HR team meetings to discuss progress, address concerns, and review key metrics.

Example: Weekly meetings to review the progress of recruitment campaigns and adjust strategies as needed. Tracking the HR and recruitment labor hours and fees for recruitment process tools required to secure an offer will help set realistic budgets in the future. Also, tracking the source of hires will help inform where to recruit from for future opportunities.

PERFORMANCE CHECK-INS

Conduct weekly performance check-ins with employees to provide ongoing support and address challenges.

Example: Weekly check-ins to discuss short-term goals, progress, and any obstacles. If staff members give you any reason to believe that they may become a flight risk, you can start having conversations with managers to improve morale or start recruiting to backfill soon-to-be vacant positions.

Monthly Activities

ENGAGEMENT SURVEYS

Conduct monthly engagement surveys to gather feedback and identify areas for improvement.

Example: Monthly surveys to track employee engagement levels and trends. If you track feedback on specific initiatives like team-building activities and training, you can understand the value that employees place on the activities while knowing the dollar amount it took to execute that activity.

TRAINING AND DEVELOPMENT

Schedule monthly training sessions or workshops on HR best practices and other relevant topics.

Example: Monthly workshops on people management skills to equip managers with necessary skills. You may be able to track which team leaders have the highest levels of engagement and see which programs had the most impact on their development.

METRICS REVIEW

Review key HR metrics such as recruitment efficiency, retention rates, and training effectiveness.

Example: Monthly analysis of time-to-fill positions, employee turnover rates, and training program feedback. This analysis will inform areas to improve team effectiveness through coaching or training programs.

Quarterly Activities

COMPREHENSIVE REVIEWS

Conduct quarterly comprehensive reviews of all HR initiatives and their impact.

Example: Quarterly reviews to assess the effectiveness of a new onboarding program based on feedback and performance data. There are strong correlations between the quality of onboarding and the tenure of a new hire. You should be able to reliably predict the tenure of a new hire based on their completion of the onboarding process, who their manager is, and the morale of their department.

STRATEGIC PLANNING

Develop a strategic plan for the next quarter, aligning HR initiatives with business goals.

Example: Quarterly planning sessions to ensure HR's alignment with organizational objectives, such as workforce planning for upcoming projects. This planning should also include budgetary considerations. How closely did your department stick to its budget? Where did you overspend and why? Where did you underspend and why?

STAKEHOLDER REPORTS

Prepare and present quarterly reports to staff and leadership summarizing HR activities and their impact.

Example: Quarterly presentations to the executive team highlighting HR's contributions to recruitment, engagement, and performance. Another example would be quarterly reminders of all benefits afforded to staff members. Reminders to spend FSA dollars, to enroll in EAP mental health services, and to take time off.

Annual Activities

ANNUAL REPORT

Prepare an annual report summarizing HR contributions, key metrics, and impact on organizational success.

Example: Annual report to demonstrate HR's value through metrics like employee retention, diversity initiatives, and leadership development outcomes. Again, can you find where HR has improved revenue or saved the company money? Seek to find ways to assert your financial value to the company, not just your operational value.

STRATEGIC REVIEW

Conduct an annual strategic review to assess the effectiveness of HR initiatives over the past year and plan for the coming year.

Example: Annual strategic review to evaluate HR's progress, set new targets for employee engagement, and outline initiatives to enhance organizational culture.

BUDGET PLANNING

Develop the HR budget for the upcoming year, justifying expenditures based on demonstrated value and strategic goals.

Example: Annual budget proposals that include funding for new HR technologies, training programs, and employee engagement initiatives.

POLICY REVIEW

Conduct an annual review of HR policies and procedures to ensure they are up-to-date and aligned with organizational goals.

Example: Annual policy audit to update employee handbooks, compliance procedures, and benefits programs.

In summary, implementing a comprehensive HR value checklist with daily, weekly, monthly, quarterly, and annual activities ensures that we stay focused, organized, and aligned with our strategic goals. By tracking and reporting our contributions consistently, we can demonstrate HR's impact and strategic value.

I encourage you to adopt and customize this checklist to fit your organization's needs. By consistently following these actions, you can showcase HR's contributions and drive organizational success.

Deep Dive: Does Your HR Strategy Measure Up?

Reflection Questions

When reflecting on the role of HR, it's important to assess how well your strategies align with the broader business goals of your organization. This alignment is critical because HR, at its best, should drive organizational success, not simply respond to it. Are your HR practices directly contributing to business objectives? If not, now is the time to recalibrate. It's your responsibility to ensure HR is integrated into the company's strategic framework and that every HR initiative is designed to move the business forward.

Metrics and measurement come next. Ask yourself, are you using the right KPIs to track HR's impact? Data is a powerful tool, but only if you're tracking the right information. You need metrics that offer actionable insights, ones you can regularly report to leadership, demonstrating HR's value in real terms. It's not enough to simply measure employee turnover or engagement—you need to know how these metrics tie back to the business's success.

Talent management plays a huge role here. How well are you attracting and retaining top talent? Your onboarding process, performance management systems, and employee feedback mechanisms are all crucial components. This is where owning your expertise comes in. You must ensure that HR is driving growth by aligning the right people with the right roles and providing them with clear, constructive feedback.

Similarly, employee engagement is key. If your workforce is disengaged, productivity and innovation will suffer. You should regularly assess employee morale, gather feedback, and take action. The value of being part coach, part cheerleader is especially relevant here. Employees want to know their work matters, and HR is in a unique position to ensure that happens by fostering a positive, engaging, high-feedback work environment.

When it comes to learning and development, you need to take a proactive approach. Are there skills gaps in your workforce? If so, you should address these through comprehensive training programs. Forward and adaptive beats static and slow—your workforce should be continuously learning, and HR should lead the charge in providing development opportunities that boost both individual and organizational performance.

Diversity, equity, inclusion, and belonging (DEIB) are fundamental to modern HR strategy. How well does your HR strategy promote DEIB, and what progress have you made so far? This is where igniting the spark comes in—HR must be a champion for DEIB, ensuring that it's not just a box to be checked but an integral part of the company's DNA. Measure your DEIB efforts with the same rigor as any other business goal, and always strive for improvement.

Communication and culture are two areas where HR's influence should be particularly strong. You need to be intentional about how HR's initiatives are communicated across the company. How well does HR communicate its goals? Bringing clarity from the clouds is essential—your role is to ensure that the organization understands HR's purpose and how it ties into the company's success. Additionally, HR should play a pivotal role in shaping and sustaining the culture, ensuring it aligns with business values and objectives.

Leveraging HR technology is no longer optional. To be effective, HR must embrace digital tools that streamline processes, enhance data analytics, and drive strategic decisions. Stay ahead of trends, explore new technologies, and use them to elevate HR's role in the business.

HR must also be flexible and adaptive. The business landscape is always shifting, and so must HR. Regularly review your strategies and ensure they remain relevant in a changing world. This adaptability is what separates HR departments that merely survive from those that truly thrive.

Finally, leadership and influence are at the heart of what makes HR successful. HR should be at the table for all strategic discussions, influencing decision-making and ensuring that people are prioritized in business planning. Owning your expertise comes into play here again—HR leaders must demonstrate their knowledge and influence, positioning HR as a critical partner in driving business success. By taking the initiative, demonstrating leadership, and being a voice of reason and progress, HR can shape the future of the organization.

In summary, the power of HR lies in its ability to align with business goals, measure its impact, foster engagement and development, promote DEI, leverage technology, adapt to change, and influence leadership decisions. HR isn't just a function—it's the engine that drives sustainable growth.

Conclusion

In conclusion, the role of HR within an organization is far more than managing people and policies—it's about driving strategic value. By aligning HR initiatives with business goals, leveraging data for decision-making, and fostering an inclusive, engaged workforce, HR can significantly contribute to an organization's success. Remember, it's not just about being reactive; it's about anticipating future needs, staying adaptable, and demonstrating how HR initiatives can create measurable impact on the bottom line.

You are at the forefront of shaping your organization's culture and future. By embracing the five HR values, you have the power to elevate HR's role and, in turn, help lead your organization to new heights.

References

Office of the U.S. Surgeon General and H. Murthy (n.d.) The U.S. Surgeon General's Framework for Workplace Mental Health & Well-Being, www.hhs.gov/sites/default/files/workplace-mental-health-well-being.pdf (archived at https://perma.cc/CRY5-QD29)

Price, J (2023) Talent & Tech: Embracing Collaboration with AI for Workplace Success, Jumpstart HR, jumpstart-hr.com/talent-tech-embracing-collaboration-with-ai-for-workplace-success-joey-price-tedxjeffersonu-collaboration-with-ai/ (archived at https://perma.cc/KJ5C-X9FP)

Segal, E (2021) Why Employees Don't Trust HR Staff—And What Can Be Done About It. Forbes, www.forbes.com/sites/edwardsegal/2021/11/28/why-employees-dont-trust-hr-staff-and-what-can-be-done-about-it/ (archived at https://perma.cc/M7YL-RA3K)

Wilkie, D (2017) Popular TV and Films Love to Hate HR, SHRM, www.shrm.org/topics-tools/news/employee-relations/popular-tv-films-love-to-hate-hr (archived at https://perma.cc/V72Y-MJSG)

3

Influencing the Business and Driving Change

Introduction

In this chapter we are going to explore one of the most impactful roles that HR can play within an organization: leading change. As HR professionals, we are uniquely positioned to drive and influence strategic change initiatives that align with our business objectives and enhance our organization's success. That is because the HR function in any organization has the power to influence policies, morale, and culture. Whether the change be large or small, we hold the power to galvanize people and facilitate change management success!

In the opening story of this chapter, our fictional HR Director Emma Thompson faces the challenge of guiding her team at Hope Haven through a post-pandemic return to the office. Through empathy, communication, and collaboration, Emma leads a successful transition that strengthens the organization's culture and highlights the transformative power of HR leadership in times of change.

Change Catalysts: HR Leaders Making a Difference

In the vibrant and diverse borough of Brooklyn, New York, the non-profit organization Hope Haven had long been a beacon of support and community development. With a dedicated team of 60 employees from various economic backgrounds and racial ethnicities, the organization had successfully transitioned to remote work during the Covid-19 pandemic. However, as the world began to recover, Hope Haven faced a new challenge: bringing its employees back to the office.

Emma Thompson, the HR Director at Hope Haven, found herself at the center of this storm. Known for her compassionate leadership and deep commitment to the organization's mission, Emma was admired by her colleagues. Yet, as the pandemic waned, she sensed a growing unease among the staff about the impending return-to-office mandate.

Emma sat in her modest office, surrounded by files and sticky notes, contemplating the daunting task ahead. She knew that simply issuing a directive wouldn't suffice; she needed to steward this change thoughtfully and empathetically. Unsure of where to start, she reached out to me for guidance.

We connected over a video call, and Emma shared her concerns. I listened carefully and then laid out a strategy. "Emma, successful change management hinges on understanding your people and aligning the change with the organization's values. You need to communicate transparently, involve your team in the process, and provide support every step of the way."

Taking this advice, Emma devised a comprehensive plan. She began by conducting anonymous surveys to gauge employees' concerns and preferences about returning to the office. The feedback was clear: many were anxious about the safety and logistics of commuting, while others had grown accustomed to the flexibility of remote work.

Armed with this information, Emma organized a series of town hall meetings to address these concerns openly. She invited a diverse panel of staff members to share their experiences and ideas for a smooth transition. These meetings fostered a sense of community and collaboration, making employees feel heard and valued.

Emma also worked closely with the facilities team to ensure that the office was equipped with enhanced safety measures, including regular sanitization, socially distanced workstations, and upgraded ventilation systems. Additionally, she negotiated flexible working hours and hybrid models to accommodate those who still needed some remote work flexibility.

To ease the transition, Emma introduced wellness programs, including mental health support and stress management workshops. She personally checked in with employees, offering a listening ear and practical assistance where needed. Her empathetic approach helped build trust and reduce resistance.

As the return-to-office date approached, the atmosphere at Hope Haven began to shift. Employees who were initially unhappy about the mandate started to feel more at ease, knowing their concerns had been addressed. The collaborative efforts had fostered a renewed sense of purpose and unity within the team.

On the first day back, Emma stood at the entrance of the office, welcoming each employee with a warm smile and a small welcome-back package. The gesture, though simple, resonated deeply with the staff. The office buzzed with cautious optimism, and over time, the team settled into the new routine, balancing in-office and remote work seamlessly.

Emma's thoughtful stewardship not only facilitated a smooth return to the office but also strengthened the organization's culture. The experience underscored a crucial lesson: HR's role in driving change is not just about enforcing policies but about leading with empathy, transparency, and a deep understanding of people.

Reflecting on the journey, Emma felt a profound sense of accomplishment. She had not only navigated a complex change but had also reinforced the values that made Hope Haven a special place to work. Her story, like many others in this book, highlights the transformative impact of HR leaders in guiding organizations through challenging times and driving positive change.

Leading Change: HR's Strategic Influence

As senior HR leaders, we must understand how to effectively lead and influence change. Our role goes beyond managing HR processes; we are key players in shaping the future direction of our organizations. In fact, according to Gartner research from 2019, there is a key change management principle that we must help our CEOs fully embrace.

"CEOs have a very important role to play in enterprise change,
but unless they establish a clear talent strategy aligned to the change,
the organization will not move quickly enough to survive." (Gartner,
2019)

Let's delve into how we can leverage our strategic influence to
lead change successfully.

Understanding the Role of HR in Leading Change

WHY HR IS CENTRAL TO CHANGE INITIATIVES

HR is at the heart of any organization because we deal directly with
the people who make up the business. Our role gives us a unique
vantage point to understand workforce dynamics, organizational
culture, and employee engagement. For instance, by regularly
conducting employee surveys and feedback sessions, HR can gauge
the overall sentiment of the workforce, identify areas of dissatisfaction, and pinpoint opportunities for improvement. This deep
understanding allows us to craft change initiatives that address the
specific needs and concerns of employees, ensuring that changes are
relevant and impactful.

Our insight into workforce dynamics positions us as critical
drivers of change. We know how different teams and departments
interact, where communication breakdowns occur, and how these
interactions affect productivity and morale. For example, if a company's sales and marketing teams are not collaborating effectively,
HR can facilitate cross-functional workshops and team-building
activities to improve communication and alignment. Additionally,
HR's role in performance management provides valuable data on
employee strengths and areas for development, enabling us to design
targeted training and development programs that support change
initiatives and build the necessary skills within the workforce.

When we lead change, we ensure that it is people-centered, sustainable, and aligned with the organization's goals. A people-centered
approach means considering the human impact of any change and

providing support throughout the transition. For instance, during a major technology upgrade, HR can offer training sessions and create resources to help employees adapt to new tools and systems. Sustainability comes from embedding change into the organizational culture, ensuring it is not just a temporary fix but a long-term improvement. By aligning change initiatives with the organization's strategic goals, such as improving customer satisfaction or increasing market share, HR ensures that these changes contribute to the broader success of the business. This alignment is crucial for gaining leadership support and demonstrating the strategic value of HR-driven change.

HR AS A STRATEGIC PARTNER

To be effective change leaders, we must be seen as strategic partners. This involves aligning our HR strategies with the broader business objectives and demonstrating how HR initiatives contribute to organizational success. By doing so, we can gain the support and trust of leadership and other stakeholders.

I should pause here to interject to answer a question that is probably on your mind: "How do I become a strategic partner when I've never been asked to participate in strategic discussions before?" That answer is simple: Build relationships before you're needed. I've mentioned this in several portions of the book thus far and it will remain a truth in later parts of the book, but leaders work with people they trust. Trust is built by investing in the relationship with your senior leadership team. Get to know their motivations, get to know their families, their personal and professional backgrounds. Whatever it takes to earn the trust of your team. The reality is that influence doesn't require a job description or place on an organizational chart. Influence is a mutual feeling where both parties trust and believe that what is said benefits all parties. You may not earn influence and trust right away but taking the time to genuinely know your senior leaders will go a long way.

Now let's discuss a few key strategies for leading change.

Key Strategies for Leading Change

DEVELOPING A CLEAR VISION AND STRATEGY

Change initiatives must start with a clear vision that outlines the desired outcomes and how they align with the organization's goals. As HR leaders, we need to articulate this vision and develop a strategic plan that includes specific objectives, timelines, and metrics for success. For example, if the goal is to improve organizational agility, our vision might include implementing flexible work arrangements, enhancing employee skills through continuous learning, and fostering a culture of innovation.

ENGAGING STAKEHOLDERS

Effective change requires the engagement and support of all stakeholders. This means involving employees at all levels, from senior leadership to frontline staff. Communication is key—clearly explaining the reasons for the change, the benefits, and how it will impact everyone involved. For example, regular town hall meetings, focus groups and feedback sessions can help ensure that everyone is on board and has a voice in the process.

CREATING A CULTURE OF CHANGE

Building a culture that embraces change is essential for long-term success. This involves fostering an environment where continuous improvement is valued and where employees feel empowered to take initiative. As HR leaders, we can promote this culture by recognizing and rewarding innovative thinking and by providing the necessary support and resources for employees to adapt to change. For instance, introducing programs that encourage cross-functional collaboration and innovation can help embed a culture of change.

IMPLEMENTING CHANGE MANAGEMENT PRACTICES

Adopting proven change management practices can significantly increase the likelihood of success. This includes conducting a thorough change impact assessment, developing a detailed implementation plan, and providing training and support to help employees navigate the transition. Utilizing frameworks like Kotter's Eight Steps for Leading Change (Kotter, 2024) can provide a structured approach to managing change. For example, setting up a change management team, creating short-term wins, and anchoring new approaches in the organization's culture are critical steps in this process.

MONITORING AND MEASURING PROGRESS

Tracking the progress of change initiatives is crucial to ensure they are on the right track and to make necessary adjustments. Establishing key performance indicators and regularly reviewing them helps to measure the impact of change efforts. For example, if the change initiative aims to improve employee engagement, metrics such as engagement survey scores, retention rates, and productivity levels can provide valuable insights into the effectiveness of the initiative.

ADDRESSING RESISTANCE

Resistance to change is natural, but it can be managed effectively. Understanding the root causes of resistance and addressing them through clear communication, empathy, and support is essential. Providing platforms for employees to express their concerns and involving them in the change process can help mitigate resistance. For example, setting up a feedback system where employees can share their thoughts and concerns anonymously can provide valuable insights into potential resistance and how to address it.

In summary, leading change requires a clear vision, strategic alignment, stakeholder engagement, a supportive culture, effective change management practices, and continuous monitoring. By leveraging these strategies, HR can play a pivotal role in driving successful change initiatives that align with organizational goals.

I encourage you to embrace your role as change leader. By strategically influencing change, we can drive meaningful improvements, enhance our organization's performance, and contribute to its long-term success.

Mentor's Corner: Overcoming HR Insecurity

How do you make the jump in your career from HR admin to HR executive? It's a common struggle that we as HR professionals face in our career. Sometimes the stumbling block is our lack of awareness of what is going on in the field around us, outside of our organization. Sometimes the stumbling block is a lack of mentorship or coaching being available in our personal or professional circles. Neither of those barriers will be a challenge for you now that you have a copy of this book in your possession.

The next Mentor's Corner conversation is with one of the most generous—and well-connected—HR professionals in our field: Lars Schmidt, Founder and CEO of Amplify Talent. Lars and I met in 2010 when my HR career was at this very crossroad—the transition from administrative expert to strategic organizational influencer. Much time has passed since then, and now we have the opportunity to talk about how you can make the jump in your own career and stay there.

The key takeaway in this section is the evolving role of HR, focusing on how HR can be a true strategic partner and not just a compliance-driven function. It can be difficult to overcome insecurities as an HR professional and step into a more proactive, impactful role—one where HR drives value for both employees and the business—but your career and organization need it.

HR's power lies in its ability to sit at the intersection of business needs and employee wellbeing. Unlike any other function, HR touches every part of the organization, and this provides a unique opportunity to shape culture, performance, and business outcomes. But to do this effectively, HR professionals need to embrace a new mindset—one that is strategic and forward-thinking.

HR has shifted over the last decade at a pace we haven't seen before. We are now able to demarcate the difference between legacy HR and modern HR. Legacy HR was often reactive, focusing on enforcing policies and managing compliance. In contrast, modern HR is proactive and deeply connected to the overall business strategy. We see HR now taking a lead role in addressing key issues like talent management, employee engagement, and even broader social issues such as diversity and inclusion. Gone are the days when HR could simply manage people; today, HR needs to be a driver of change, helping to shape the future of work.

One of the critical themes that you should know about is the decentralization of power in the HR department and HR bodies of knowledge more globally. Historically, HR teams often felt that retaining control over decision-making gave them more influence within the company. But, in reality, this approach only led to bottlenecks, frustration, and an overly bureaucratic process that alienated employees. The real power of HR comes from creating frameworks that empower managers and leaders to make decisions while ensuring that those decisions align with the company's values and strategy. It's about letting go of the need to control everything and trusting the broader organization to operate within the systems HR creates.

Lars and I both agree that one of the biggest shifts in HR is the embracing of **risk**. Legacy HR was about minimizing risk and avoiding potential problems at all costs. Modern HR, on the other hand, embraces creativity and innovation, even when it means taking calculated risks. Whether it's experimenting with new tools like AI, rethinking workplace policies in the wake of a global pandemic, or finding ways to better support a multigenerational workforce, HR must be at the forefront of change, rather than playing catch-up.

A great example of this new, risk-taking HR approach is the shift away from blanket policies aimed at preventing worst-case scenarios. Traditional HR policies were often written with a "policy against the few" mindset, meaning policies were designed to guard against the rare employee who might act inappropriately. The problem with this approach is that it punishes the majority of employees who are responsible and trustworthy. Modern HR, however, takes a "policy for the many" approach, assuming that employees are capable of making good decisions and addressing issues on an individual basis as they arise. This shift empowers employees and creates a more flexible, agile work environment. If you were to take inventory of your organization's policies, are they more aligned with legacy HR or modern HR?

HR's role has also expanded beyond just managing people to becoming talent architects. Lars has seen the workforce change dramatically in recent years. We now have six generations working together, each with unique needs and expectations. In addition, the rise of the gig economy, coupled with rapid technological advancements like AI, means that HR leaders must think more creatively about how they structure teams and deploy talent.

The definition of talent itself has evolved to include not just full-time employees but also project-based workers, freelancers, and even AI. HR professionals today must be able to assess what talent is needed for each project or business objective, while also integrating technology to handle routine tasks. It's no longer about finding full-time employees to fill every role—it's about creating a flexible, dynamic workforce that can adapt to the business's ever-changing needs.

Another powerful shift Lars emphasizes is the importance of learning agility. HR professionals can no longer afford to specialize in just one area like recruiting or employee engagement. We need to have a deep understanding of the business, technology, and broader societal trends that impact the workforce. This means continuously learning, staying curious, and making time for professional development, even when it feels like there's no time.

Building network equity is another key theme you will want to explore. It's not enough to have expertise in your own domain—you need to cultivate a network of professionals who can provide you with insights, ideas, and support. This network, or what Lars calls "collective intellect," gives HR leaders the ability to tap into the experiences and knowledge of others, enabling them to solve problems more effectively and bring innovative solutions to their organizations.

Applying the Five HR Values

Now, let's talk about how the five HR values I've outlined in this book align to give you the power to move from HR of old to HR of the here and now.

OWN YOUR EXPERTISE

HR's role is no longer just about managing people—it's about shaping the future of work. To do this effectively, you need to own your expertise. This means understanding not just HR but also the business, technology, and external factors that impact your organization. HR leaders who take the time to continuously learn and grow their knowledge will be the ones who drive real change within their companies.

BE PART COACH, PART CHEERLEADER

The importance of decentralizing power and empowering managers to lead their teams cannot be stated enough. As an HR leader, you need to be both a coach and a cheerleader. This means guiding managers and employees, helping them grow and succeed, while also being their biggest advocate. When HR plays this dual role, it creates a more engaged, empowered workforce. It also empowers managers to form deeper relationships with their employees because they will be seen as the problem solvers in the organization and not just HR.

IGNITE THE SPARK

If you want to fully tap into the power of HR, you must embrace creativity and innovation. Whether it's experimenting with new technologies like AI or rethinking workplace policies, HR leaders have the opportunity to ignite the spark of innovation within their organizations. By creating an environment where employees feel empowered to take risks and think creatively, we can drive both engagement and business results.

BRING CLARITY FROM THE CLOUDS

HR leaders in modern HR environments simplify complex issues and provide clear, actionable solutions. Whether you're managing workplace transformation or addressing the needs of a multigenerational workforce, HR's role is to bring clarity to the situation. This means breaking down problems into manageable pieces, communicating clearly with leadership and employees, and ensuring that everyone understands the path forward.

FORWARD AND ADAPTIVE BEATS STATIC AND SLOW

The world of work is changing rapidly, and HR must be at the fore-front of this transformation. Whether it's navigating the rise of the gig economy, integrating AI into the workforce, or addressing the needs of a diverse, multigenerational team, HR leaders need to be forward-thinking and adaptable. The companies that succeed in the future will be the ones with HR teams that can anticipate change and respond with agility.

Conclusion

In today's fast-evolving business landscape, HR's value lies in its ability to shape the future of work. By owning our expertise, empowering managers and employees, embracing innovation, simplifying complex issues, and staying agile, HR leaders can drive both employee engagement and business success.

Lars and I agree on one fundamental point: HR professionals can no longer afford to be reactive. They need to take the lead in transforming their organizations by aligning HR initiatives with business goals, fostering a culture of creativity and adaptability, and driving change from the ground up.

By applying the five HR values in your everyday work, you'll not only demonstrate the true power of HR but also position yourself as a strategic partner who can help your organization thrive in the years to come.

Difficult Dynamics: Navigating Resistance in Change

Change is an inevitable part of growth and progress, yet it often meets with resistance. Let's discuss the difficult dynamics of navigating resistance in change. Understanding these dynamics is crucial for HR professionals who are at the forefront of driving and managing change within organizations.

As senior HR leaders, we are tasked with not only implementing change but also addressing the resistance that comes with it. Our role requires us to navigate these challenges strategically to ensure that change initiatives are successful and sustainable. Let's explore the complexities of resistance and the strategies we can employ to overcome it.

Understanding the Nature of Resistance

WHY RESISTANCE OCCURS

Resistance to change is a natural reaction that can stem from various sources. Fear of the unknown, loss of control, and disruption of routines are common reasons why employees may resist change. For example, when introducing a new technology platform, employees might worry about their ability to learn and adapt to the new system. Understanding these underlying fears and concerns is the first step in addressing resistance.

TYPES OF RESISTANCE

Resistance can manifest in different ways—overtly through vocal opposition and protests, or covertly through passive behaviors such as decreased productivity and low morale. For instance, during a restructuring process, some employees might openly express their dissatisfaction, while others might quietly disengage from their work. Recognizing the different forms of resistance allows us to tailor our approach to effectively manage and mitigate it.

IMPACT OF RESISTANCE

Unchecked resistance can significantly derail change initiatives, leading to delays, increased costs, and even failure. It can also create a negative work environment, affecting overall employee morale and productivity. Therefore, it's essential to address resistance proactively and constructively to maintain momentum and achieve the desired outcomes.

Strategies for Navigating Resistance

EFFECTIVE COMMUNICATION

Clear and transparent communication is crucial in managing resistance. Keeping employees informed about the reasons for the change, the benefits, and the expected outcomes helps alleviate fears and build trust. For example, regular town hall meetings, detailed email updates, and an open-door policy for questions can ensure that employees feel included and valued in the process. Providing a platform for employees to voice their concerns and receive honest responses is key to fostering a culture of openness.

INVOLVEMENT AND PARTICIPATION

Engaging employees in the change process increases their sense of ownership and reduces resistance. Involving them in planning and decision-making can lead to more innovative solutions and smoother implementation. For instance, creating cross-functional teams to work on change initiatives or soliciting feedback through focus groups can help employees feel more connected and invested in the change. This participatory approach not only addresses resistance but also leverages the collective expertise of the workforce.

PROVIDING SUPPORT AND RESOURCES

Offering the necessary support and resources to help employees adapt to change is essential. This can include training programs, coaching, and access to new tools and technologies. For example, when implementing a new software system, providing comprehensive training sessions, user manuals, and a dedicated helpdesk can ease the transition and build confidence among employees. Ensuring that support is ongoing, rather than one-time, helps sustain the change.

ADDRESSING EMOTIONAL RESPONSES

Change often triggers emotional responses such as fear, anxiety, and frustration. Acknowledging these emotions and addressing them with empathy is crucial. Providing counseling services, stress management workshops, and one-on-one sessions with managers can help employees navigate their emotional responses. For instance, during a major organizational restructuring, offering support groups and individual counseling can help employees cope with uncertainty and loss.

MONITORING AND ADJUSTING

Continuous monitoring and flexibility in the change process are vital. Regularly assessing the impact of change initiatives and being willing to make adjustments based on feedback can mitigate resistance. For example, conducting pulse surveys and feedback sessions can provide real-time insights into employee sentiments, allowing for timely interventions. Demonstrating a willingness to adapt the approach based on feedback reinforces the commitment to a successful and inclusive change process.

In summary, navigating resistance in change requires a deep understanding of its nature, effective communication, involvement and participation, providing support and resources, addressing emotional responses, and continuous monitoring. By employing these strategies, HR can successfully lead change initiatives and minimize resistance.

I encourage you to apply these strategies in your organization and apply them in your change initiatives. By proactively managing resistance, you can ensure that your efforts lead to successful and sustainable outcomes.

CASE STUDY EXERCISE

Navigating Resistance During Cost-Cutting Measures

You are the HR Director at a mid-sized manufacturing company, Precision Tools Inc. The company is experiencing a financial downturn due to a decline in sales and increased production costs. Senior leadership has decided that significant cost-cutting measures are necessary to stabilize the company's finances. These measures include reducing departmental budgets, implementing a hiring freeze, and introducing mandatory unpaid leave for all employees. As the HR Director, you are responsible for managing the implementation of these changes and addressing the inevitable resistance from employees.

Please note: This case study is entirely fictitious. Any relationship to a real-world organization or person is entirely coincidental.

Task

Develop a strategy to navigate and address the objections and resistance from employees regarding the cost-cutting measures. Your strategy should include clear communication plans, engagement activities, and support mechanisms to help employees understand and cope with the changes.

Supporting Questions

- What are the likely objections and concerns employees may have about the cost-cutting measures?

- How might these objections differ among various departments and employee groups (e.g., production staff vs. office staff)?

- What key messages need to be communicated to employees about the reasons for the cost-cutting measures?

- What channels (e.g., town hall meetings, emails, one-on-one meetings) will you use to communicate these messages?

- How can you involve employees in the change process to increase their sense of ownership and reduce resistance?

Influence Checklist: Key Activities for HR Leaders

As HR leaders, our ability to influence the organization and drive strategic initiatives is crucial. This checklist provides key actions broken down into daily, weekly, monthly, quarterly, and annual tasks to enhance your influence and ensure your HR strategies are aligned with business objectives.

Daily Activities

UNDERSTAND THE BUSINESS

- Stay informed: Read daily industry news and company updates to stay informed about the business environment.

BUILD STRONG RELATIONSHIPS

- Network internally: Engage in brief, informal conversations with colleagues and employees to build rapport.

COMMUNICATE EFFECTIVELY

- Be approachable: Maintain an open-door policy to encourage communication and trust.
- Listen actively: Practice active listening in all interactions to understand needs and concerns.

DRIVE CHANGE

- Lead by example: Exhibit behaviors and attitudes that support ongoing change initiatives.

Weekly Activities

UNDERSTAND THE BUSINESS

- Review metrics: Analyze weekly performance metrics to stay updated on key business indicators.

BUILD STRONG RELATIONSHIPS

- Regular check-ins: Schedule and conduct regular check-ins with department heads and team leaders.

COMMUNICATE EFFECTIVELY

- Team meetings: Hold weekly team meetings to discuss ongoing projects, share updates, and gather feedback.
- Transparent communication: Provide updates on HR initiatives and changes.

DRIVE CHANGE

- Engage employees: Identify opportunities to involve employees in change processes through feedback sessions or suggestion boxes.

DEVELOP HR EXPERTISE

- Learning and development: Dedicate time to read HR articles, attend webinars, or listen to industry podcasts.

Monthly Activities

UNDERSTAND THE BUSINESS

- Analyze financials: Review monthly financial reports to understand the company's financial health.

BUILD STRONG RELATIONSHIPS

- Networking events: Attend internal or external networking events to build relationships and gather insights.

COMMUNICATE EFFECTIVELY

- Monthly reports: Prepare and distribute monthly HR reports to highlight achievements and ongoing initiatives.
- Use data and stories: Combine data-driven insights with compelling stories in communications.

DEMONSTRATE STRATEGIC VALUE

- Measure impact: Evaluate the effectiveness of HR initiatives and report on their impact using metrics.

DEVELOP HR EXPERTISE

- Certifications and training: Enroll in or complete relevant HR certification courses or training programs.

Quarterly Activities

UNDERSTAND THE BUSINESS

- Strategic reviews: Participate in quarterly business strategy meetings to align HR initiatives with business goals.

BUILD STRONG RELATIONSHIPS

- Leadership meetings: Schedule quarterly meetings with senior leadership to discuss HR's strategic role.

COMMUNICATE EFFECTIVELY

- Quarterly updates: Present quarterly updates to senior leadership on HR's contributions and progress.
- Feedback sessions: Conduct feedback sessions with employees to gather insights and improve HR practices.

DRIVE CHANGE

- Change management: Review and adjust change management strategies based on quarterly progress assessments.

LEVERAGE TECHNOLOGY

- HR analytics: Use HR analytics tools to track and report on key HR metrics and trends.

Annual Activities

UNDERSTAND THE BUSINESS

- Annual strategy planning: Participate in annual strategic planning sessions to align HR strategies with long-term business objectives.

BUILD STRONG RELATIONSHIPS

- Employee surveys: Conduct an annual employee engagement survey to gather comprehensive feedback.

COMMUNICATE EFFECTIVELY

- Annual report: Prepare an annual HR report summarizing key achievements, challenges, and strategic plans.

DEMONSTRATE STRATEGIC VALUE

- Review metrics: Conduct an annual review of all HR metrics to evaluate overall impact and areas for improvement.

DRIVE CHANGE

- Reflect and plan: Reflect on the past year's change initiatives and plan new strategies for the upcoming year.

DEVELOP HR EXPERTISE

- Benchmarking: Perform annual benchmarking against industry standards to ensure best practices in HR.

LEVERAGE TECHNOLOGY

- Tech review: Review and assess HR technology solutions annually to ensure they meet evolving needs and industry standards.

This structured checklist ensures that you consistently engage in activities that build influence, align HR initiatives with business goals, and demonstrate your strategic value. By breaking down actions into daily, weekly, monthly, quarterly, and annual activities, you can maintain focus, drive continuous improvement, and enhance your impact.

> I encourage you to adopt and customize this checklist to fit your organization's needs. By consistently following these actions, you can showcase HR's contributions and drive organizational success.

Reflecting on Influence: Your Role in Organizational Dynamics

As an HR leader, your ability to influence organizational dynamics is crucial to both your success and the success of the company. Influence doesn't just come from your title—it comes from your strategic alignment with the business, your ability to lead change, and your power to engage and motivate employees and leadership alike. Reflecting on how you demonstrate influence can provide valuable insights into your current role and how you can enhance your impact.

One of the most significant ways HR can drive influence is by ensuring that your initiatives are closely aligned with the organization's business goals. It's not enough to run programs or offer solutions that only benefit employees; these initiatives must also drive strategic objectives, like revenue growth, efficiency, or innovation. Ask yourself: how often do you review your HR strategies to make sure they support the broader goals of the company? If there are gaps, what steps can you take to tighten that alignment? Every decision you make should link back to how it serves the company's future—whether it's talent management, employee engagement, or organizational development.

Let's also discuss the role of owning your expertise in influencing decision-making. HR's power lies in the deep understanding of both people and business strategy. When HR leaders take the time to truly understand their company's financials, market positioning, and competitive landscape, they can offer insights that go beyond typical HR functions. When you bring that level of expertise to the table, you're not just influencing HR outcomes—you're shaping business decisions. Be proactive in sharing data and insights that connect employee performance and engagement to business outcomes. This not only builds your credibility but also solidifies HR as a strategic partner.

Change is inevitable in any organization, and HR's role in driving and managing that change is paramount. When considering your influence, ask yourself how effectively you've managed recent changes within the organization. Did you simply implement what was asked, or did you take an active role in shaping the change? Being part coach, part cheerleader means guiding both leadership and employees through transitions, ensuring everyone is aligned on why the change is happening and how it benefits the business. When you communicate change clearly and show how it serves the company's objectives, you help reduce resistance and increase buy-in.

However, managing change isn't just about implementation—it's also about bringing clarity from the clouds. HR often deals with complex and ambiguous situations, whether it's navigating workplace transformations, addressing multigenerational workforce needs, or introducing new technology like AI. Your role is to break down these challenges into clear, actionable steps for both leadership and employees. Simplifying the complexity not only demonstrates your leadership but also ensures that everyone can follow the path forward with confidence. Strong, clear communication is critical here—without it, even the best-intentioned changes can falter.

Relationship-building is another critical aspect of demonstrating influence. HR cannot operate in a vacuum; your success is closely tied to how well you collaborate with senior leadership, managers, and employees. Think about your current relationships with key stakeholders—are they strong enough to support your initiatives? Are you seen as a trusted advisor, or simply as a functionary? Strong relationships help build the trust you need to influence change effectively. Consider adopting forward and adaptive beats static and slow by continuously seeking feedback and evolving your approach to relationships. When you maintain adaptability in your interactions, you stay relevant and demonstrate that HR is not just reactive but proactive in meeting organizational needs.

Influence doesn't stop with implementing change—it's also about measuring the impact of your initiatives. Igniting the spark within an organization is only effective when it can be sustained, and this requires tracking metrics that demonstrate the long-term benefits of your efforts. What KPIs are you using to measure success? More importantly, how do you communicate those results back to leadership? Reporting the tangible outcomes of HR-led initiatives, whether through improved employee retention, increased engagement, or higher productivity, shows that HR is not just a cost center—it's a driving force behind the company's success.

Lastly, reflection is essential to continuously improve your influence. As an HR leader, it's important to evaluate not only your successes but also the areas where you can grow. Where can you develop further? Are you making time for professional development, and are you learning from others in your field? HR is evolving quickly, and staying on top of new trends, technologies, and strategies will keep you relevant and impactful. Consider building network equity by engaging with peers outside your direct domain—this gives you access to a wealth of shared experiences and knowledge that you can bring back to your organization.

In summary, demonstrating HR's influence comes down to strategic alignment, strong communication, relationship-building, and continuous learning. By applying the five HR values—Own Your Expertise; Be Part Coach, Part Cheerleader; Ignite the Spark; Bring Clarity From the Clouds; and Forward and Adaptive Beats Static and Slow—you not only solidify your role within the organization but also ensure that HR is seen as a strategic driver of business success. Whether you're leading change, aligning HR with business goals, or managing complex dynamics, your influence is critical in shaping both the workforce and the future of the organization.

Conclusion

As you reflect on the insights from this chapter, remember that HR is more than a support function—it's a strategic driver of organizational success. Leading change requires a delicate balance of empathy, clear communication, and unwavering commitment to aligning HR initiatives with business objectives. When HR leads with these principles, it not only fosters smoother transitions but also creates lasting improvements in culture and performance. Embrace your role as a change leader, and continue to develop the skills, relationships, and strategies that will elevate HR's influence across your organization. The future of your company starts with HR.

References

Gartner (2019) Three Change Conversations Every CEO Must Have with the Head of HR, Gartner, Inc, www.gartner.com/en/human-resources/trends/3-change-conversations-every-ceo-must-have-with-the-head-of-hr (archived at https://perma.cc/6XCB-KMFT)

Kotter, J (2024) The 8 Steps for Leading Change, Kotter International Inc, www.kotterinc.com/methodology/8-steps/ (archived at https://perma.cc/WX6Q-SWB4)

4

The Importance of Data, Analytics, and Evidence for HR

Introduction

In an era where data reigns supreme, HR professionals are being called upon to embrace analytics as a key component of strategic decision-making. Gone are the days when HR's primary role was transactional; today, HR is expected to drive business outcomes by interpreting and leveraging data to influence workforce decisions.

In this chapter, we will explore how HR analytics can be a game-changer for organizations, using real-world examples and practical insights. From assessing skills gaps to designing effective training programs, data-driven decision-making empowers HR leaders to lead with precision and foresight. The power of evidence-based HR practices is undeniable—it improves transparency, enhances decision-making, and builds trust across the organization. Whether you're navigating technological disruptions like AI in the workplace or managing talent to align with strategic goals, HR analytics is the key to making informed decisions that drive business success.

Sophia Martinez, HR Manager at Last Mile Express, is at the heart of a fictional tale that illustrates the power of data-driven HR strategies. Tasked with identifying skills gaps to prevent job losses from AI automation, Sophia uses workforce analytics to upskill employees. Through her strategic approach, she ensures the company stays competitive while safeguarding jobs. This story exemplifies how HR can leverage data and analytics to lead organizations through transformative change, demonstrating the value of proactive decision-making in a rapidly evolving industry.

Data-Driven Decisions: HR's New Frontier

In Utah, Last Mile Express, a last-mile delivery business employing 1,000 dedicated workers, faced a significant challenge. As technological advances, particularly in artificial intelligence, began to reshape the industry, the company needed to identify skills gaps and upskill workers who risked being replaced by AI.

Sophia Martinez, the HR Manager at Last Mile Express, was entrusted with this daunting task. Known for her analytical mind and commitment to her team, Sophia understood the gravity of the situation. If she could successfully navigate this challenge, she would not only secure the futures of many employees but also strengthen the company's competitive edge.

One morning, Sophia sat in her office, reviewing the CEO's directive. She had to create a process to capture the current skills within the workforce, implement a comprehensive training program, and measure the results to ensure business success. Unsure where to start, she reached out to me for some strategic guidance.

We connected over a video call, and I listened as Sophia detailed her challenges. I shared insights on how data and analytics could be pivotal in addressing her needs. "Sophia, the first step is to gather accurate data on your employees' current skill sets. Then, you can identify the gaps and design a targeted upskilling program. Finally, measure the outcomes to demonstrate the value of your initiatives."

Sophia took this advice and began by deploying a company-wide skills assessment survey. She collaborated with department heads to ensure the survey captured a comprehensive picture of the workforce's capabilities. The data revealed several critical gaps, particularly in areas susceptible to automation.

With this information in hand, Sophia designed a multifaceted training program focused on upskilling and reskilling employees. She partnered with a local technical institute to offer courses in data analysis, machine learning, and advanced logistics management. To make learning accessible, she implemented a blended approach, combining online modules with in-person workshops.

Sophia also developed a robust system to track progress. Using HR analytics software, she monitored enrollment rates, course completion, and post-training performance. She created dashboards to visualize this data, making it easy to identify trends and areas needing additional support.

The training program was met with enthusiasm and some skepticism. To address this, Sophia organized town hall meetings to communicate the importance of upskilling and how it would secure their jobs in an evolving industry. She shared success stories and highlighted the long-term benefits of continuous learning.

As months passed, the impact of Sophia's initiatives became evident. Employees who completed the training showed marked improvements in their performance and adaptability.

Encouraged by these results, the leadership team at Last Mile Express decided to expand the training program. They invested in advanced training modules and continuous learning opportunities, embedding a culture of development within the company.

Sophia's data-driven approach not only addressed the immediate challenge but also positioned Last Mile Express as an industry leader in employee development. Her work underscored a vital lesson: leveraging data and analytics is crucial for making informed HR decisions that drive business success.

Reflecting on the journey, Sophia felt a profound sense of accomplishment. She had not only safeguarded the livelihoods of her colleagues but had also demonstrated the transformative power of data-driven HR practices. Her story, like many others in this book, highlights how strategic use of data and analytics can propel HR into a new frontier of business impact.

The Power of Evidence: Using Data to Support HR Decisions

In a world increasingly driven by data, using evidence to support HR decisions is no longer a luxury, it is a necessity. Evidence-based HR practices help us make informed decisions that align with organizational goals and drive performance.

As senior HR professionals, our role extends beyond traditional HR functions. We are strategic partners who influence key business decisions in the era of Big Data and Generative AI. Through leveraging data and evidence, we can enhance our credibility, demonstrate the impact of our initiatives, and contribute more effectively to the success of our organizations. Let's explore how we can harness the power of evidence to support our HR decisions.

Understanding Evidence-Based HR

DEFINITION AND IMPORTANCE

Evidence-based HR involves making decisions informed by data, research, and empirical evidence rather than intuition or anecdotal information. This approach allows us to objectively evaluate the effectiveness of our HR practices and make adjustments based on what the data tells us. For instance, rather than relying on gut feelings to determine the success of a new training program, we can use data on employee performance and feedback to assess its impact.

KEY BENEFITS

The benefits of evidence-based HR are numerous. It enhances decision-making accuracy, improves transparency, and builds trust with stakeholders by providing a clear rationale for HR initiatives. Additionally, it enables us to identify trends, predict outcomes, and develop strategies that are grounded in solid evidence. For example, analyzing turnover data can help us identify patterns and develop targeted retention strategies.

The benefits of evidence-based HR are widely documented. In 2021, Oracle partnered with HR.com's HR Research Institute to produce *The State of HR Analytics in 2021* (Oracle and the HR Research Institute, 2021). Among several other major findings, the research found that HR analytics-leader firms are ten times more likely to be effective at providing insights to top leaders. In short, your ability to analyze HR and non-HR data to inform business decisions will increase the value you bring to the organization.

Implementing Evidence-Based HR Practices

DATA COLLECTION

The first step in implementing evidence-based HR is to collect relevant data. This includes quantitative data such as employee performance metrics, turnover rates, and engagement scores, as well as qualitative data like employee feedback and exit interview insights. Ensuring that we have accurate and comprehensive data is crucial. For instance, regularly conducting employee surveys can provide valuable insights into workplace morale and satisfaction.

DATA ANALYSIS

Once we have collected the data, the next step is to analyze it to uncover insights and trends. Utilizing HR analytics tools can help us make sense of complex data sets and identify actionable insights. For example, by analyzing recruitment data, we can determine which sourcing channels yield the best candidates and adjust our recruitment strategies accordingly. Advanced analytics techniques, such as predictive analytics, can even help us forecast future HR needs and trends.

MAKING DATA-DRIVEN DECISIONS

With the insights gained from data analysis, we can make informed, evidence-based decisions. This involves interpreting the data in the context of our organizational goals and using it to guide our HR strategies. For example, if data shows that certain training programs lead to higher employee performance, we can allocate more resources to those programs. Additionally, by setting up key performance indicators and regularly tracking progress, we can ensure that our decisions are yielding the desired results.

Communicating the Value of Evidence-Based Decisions

BUILDING CREDIBILITY

Communicating the value of evidence-based decisions to stakeholders is essential. By presenting data and evidence to support our HR initiatives, we can build credibility and gain buy-in from leadership and employees. For instance, when proposing a new employee wellness program, presenting data on the positive impact of similar programs in other organizations can strengthen our case.

Transparency in our decision-making process also helps build trust and demonstrates our commitment to making informed, objective decisions. How do we incorporate transparency in the decision-making process? Communicate not only the decisions but the factors that went into evaluating and arriving at the decisions. Also, don't forget to incorporate collaboration where possible.

STORYTELLING WITH DATA

Effective communication involves not just presenting data but also telling a compelling story with it. Using visual aids such as charts, graphs, and dashboards can make data more accessible and understandable. For example, creating a visual dashboard that tracks key HR metrics over time can help stakeholders easily see the impact of HR initiatives. By combining data with real-life examples and narratives, we can make a more persuasive case for our decisions.

In summary, evidence-based HR practices are essential for making informed, effective decisions that align with organizational goals. By collecting and analyzing relevant data, making data-driven decisions, and effectively communicating the value of these decisions, we can enhance our strategic impact and drive better outcomes for our organizations.

> I encourage you to embrace the power of evidence in your HR practices. By leveraging data and evidence to support your decisions, you can enhance your credibility, improve your decision-making accuracy, and contribute more effectively to your organization's success.

Mentor's Corner: How HR Analytics, Workplace Investigations, and HR Tech Are Influencing Today's Workplace

When it comes to understanding how HR analytics is evolving and impacting organizations, there is a holistic conversation that must be had. Yes, analytics matter in the traditional sense of data and technology, but what about data collection in workplace investigations? My conversations with Richard Rosenow (VP, People Analytics Strategy at One Model), Kate Bischoff (Attorney and HR Consultant at k8bisch, LLC), and Madeline Laurano (Founder at Aptitude Research) offered a wealth of perspectives on what it means to truly harness the power of analytics, technology, and data-driven strategies in HR. Each expert brought their own unique viewpoint on how HR leaders can leverage analytics to make more informed decisions and drive organizational success.

Analytics as a Strategic Function

In my conversation with Richard Rosenow, he emphasized that people analytics is still a growing field. It's not fully mature, and that's okay—it means there is room for HR professionals to experiment, learn, and innovate. Richard envisions the field of HR analytics as a movement, a community, and an act. The movement is the focus we have in modern work culture on harnessing the power of technology at scale. The community is made up of people passionate about changing how we make workforce decisions using data. The act of people analytics involves everyone in the company, not just the HR team, using data to guide decision-making.

Richard's insight was that people analytics is not just about tracking numbers; it's about understanding which metrics drive business outcomes and how you can use those insights to steer the company forward. Too often, HR teams focus on the wrong metrics—those that sound important but don't really move the needle for the business. The key is identifying the metrics that genuinely impact business goals. As Richard said, "If I pull lever A, outcome B changes." That's the kind of correlation HR leaders need to find in their data. However,

Richard also acknowledged that many organizations struggle to align their HR analytics with broader business objectives. The solution? A mindset shift. HR must focus on strategy first, and then use analytics as a tool to execute that strategy effectively.

Ethics and the Power of HR in Investigations

My conversation with attorney Kate Bischoff took us into the realm of HR investigations, which are critical moments where data can be used to protect an organization and its people. Kate emphasized the importance of maintaining ethics and objectivity during investigations, noting that investigations are about fact-finding, not fault-finding.

Kate has a strong belief that HR leaders should "outsource their credibility" when necessary. In other words, know when to own the burden of fact-finding and decision-making and when to delegate that to outside counsel. This is not a sales pitch, it is good business for the organization and your professional reputation. One of Kate's rules to abide by as an internal HR leader? If you're investigating someone at your level or above, it's often best to bring in an external investigator. By doing so, you maintain your objectivity and avoid risking your reputation.

Kate also wants you to know that data must be used ethically in investigations. Employee data must be handled carefully to respect privacy. In today's world, HR professionals must be vigilant about how they collect, store, and use data, especially with the rise of AI. When done right, HR investigations safeguard both the company and its culture, helping to uphold organizational integrity.

HR Tech and the Role of Analytics in the Employee Experience

Madeline Laurano, Founder of Aptitude Research, is a leading evaluator of HR technology. What does she emphasize as critical for all HR leaders to know? How modern tech empowers HR professionals to focus on more strategic initiatives. In the past, HR technology was primarily used to manage workflows, store data, or process payroll.

But today, technology enables HR to play a far more strategic role. AI and automation take over much of the administrative burden, freeing HR leaders to focus on relationship-building and creating a better employee experience.

Another critical point you should know is that there is increasing involvement of C-level executives in HR tech decisions. That's right, the CEO wants to know how your next HRIS implementation will drive transformational progress towards business objectives! With technology budgets growing and AI becoming more central to the conversation, HR professionals must be ready to guide these discussions. In what ways are you learning to become technologically savvy beyond the apps on your phone?

Lastly, Madeline wants you to know that the integration of HR systems is critical to keep labor costs manageable and data integrity high. When systems don't talk to each other, it creates extra work and a disjointed experience for employees. In my opinion, this is the most important takeaway when evaluating your HR tech stack. The ability to transfer data from one point of entry to several outputs is a major win for modern HR leaders who take pride in the credibility of HR customer service. HR technology, when leveraged correctly, not only improves efficiency but also enhances the overall employee experience, helping employees grow and develop within the organization.

Applying the Five HR Values to HR Analytics and Tech

Throughout these conversations, the five core HR values emerged as pivotal in applying HR analytics and tech in a way that truly demonstrates the value of HR to an organization. Here's how these values align with the insights from Richard, Kate, and Madeline.

OWN YOUR EXPERTISE

HR analytics requires HR leaders to step up as experts not just in people management but in data interpretation and strategy. Richard's emphasis on the connection between metrics and business outcomes illustrates this perfectly. It's not enough to collect data; HR leaders must own their expertise in analyzing it and translating those insights into actionable strategies that drive the business forward. Madeline's insights on HR tech further underscore this point. Technology is there to empower HR, but only if you fully understand its capabilities and how to apply them strategically. Being the go-to expert on both HR and analytics sets you apart as a key decision-maker in the company.

BE PART COACH, PART CHEERLEADER

In leading investigations or managing employee relations, HR must balance being a coach and a cheerleader. Kate's discussion on ethical investigations highlighted how HR can guide the process while ensuring fairness. HR professionals often find themselves coaching leaders on how to handle sensitive situations, while also cheering on the organization's commitment to integrity and ethical behavior. This dual role is essential when implementing HR analytics as well—leaders need coaching on how to use data, and employees need encouragement that analytics are being used to create a fairer, more transparent workplace.

IGNITE THE SPARK

HR analytics is all about igniting the spark of innovation within your organization. Richard's idea of "pulling levers" to achieve business outcomes through people data is a powerful example of how analytics can be used to drive meaningful change. Whether it's finding the right metric that influences productivity or using data to identify talent gaps, HR's ability to innovate with data can transform the way the business operates. Similarly, Madeline's insights into HR tech show how technology can spark new ways of working, from automating administrative tasks to creating more personalized employee experiences.

BRING CLARITY FROM THE CLOUDS

Both Richard and Kate emphasized the importance of clarity when using data. In analytics, it's not about gathering as much data as possible; it's about making sure that data brings clarity to decision-making. Richard spoke about identifying the right metrics that actually drive business outcomes. Meanwhile, Kate's perspective highlights how data can be used to establish credibility in investigations. HR professionals must take on the role of bringing clarity—whether through data or through investigations—so that leaders and employees alike understand the path forward.

FORWARD AND ADAPTIVE BEATS STATIC AND SLOW

Madeline's insights on HR tech perfectly encapsulate this value. The world of HR is changing rapidly, especially with the rise of AI and automation. HR leaders must be forward-thinking and adaptable, embracing new technologies and methods to stay ahead. Madeline noted that C-level executives are now more involved in HR tech decisions than ever before. HR leaders need to be ready to guide those conversations and ensure the technology they adopt is not only forward-thinking but also integrated and scalable. The days of static, one-size-fits-all solutions are over—HR must be agile and ready to adapt to the changing needs of both the business and its people.

Conclusion

Richard Rosenow, Kate Bischoff, and Madeline Laurano offer rich insights into how HR can leverage analytics, technology, and ethics to drive organizational success. From understanding which metrics truly matter to ensuring ethical use of employee data, these expert insights provide valuable guidance on how HR can make a real impact. By applying the five HR values—Own Your Expertise; Be Part Coach, Part Cheerleader; Ignite the Spark; Bring Clarity From the Clouds; and Forward and Adaptive Beats Static and Slow—HR leaders can not only demonstrate their value but also lead their organizations through transformative change.

HR analytics and tech are powerful tools, but they are only as effective as the strategies and values behind them. That's where your power comes in! As HR professionals, we must continuously refine our approach, ensuring that everything we do drives the business forward while staying true to the people we serve. By embracing these principles, HR can remain at the forefront of organizational success.

CASE STUDY EXERCISE

Using HR Analytics in Employee Investigation for Compliance Audit

You are the HR Director at Tech Innovators Inc., a tech company that recently implemented a hybrid work policy requiring all employees to work in the office three days a week. After three months, you've discovered inconsistencies in the enforcement of this policy. Some managers are strictly enforcing the rule, while others are not, leading to confusion and non-compliance among employees. As part of the company's progressive disciplinary program, you need to assess compliance using HR analytics, identify which employees need to be written up, and coach the managers who are not consistently enforcing the policy.

    Please note: This case study is entirely fictitious. Any relationship to a real-world organization or person is entirely coincidental.

Task

Develop a strategy to conduct a compliance audit using HR analytics and follow through with the necessary disciplinary actions and managerial coaching. Your strategy should include steps for collecting and analyzing data, identifying non-compliant employees, implementing disciplinary actions, and coaching managers on consistent policy enforcement.

Supporting Questions

- What data will you need to collect to assess compliance with the in-office work policy?

- What metrics will you use to determine compliance or non-compliance?

- How will you identify managers who are not consistently enforcing the in-office work policy?

- What coaching techniques will you use to help these managers understand the importance of consistent policy enforcement?

- What communication strategies will you employ to reinforce the importance of this policy to all employees and managers?

HR Analytics Checklist: Must-Do Measures

Utilizing evidence-based practices and conducting thorough investigations is crucial for effective HR management. This checklist outlines daily, weekly, monthly, quarterly, and annual activities to ensure your HR decisions are data-driven and investigations are thorough.

Daily Activities

DATA COLLECTION

- Monitor attendance: Track employee attendance and time logs.
- Employee feedback: Collect daily feedback through pulse surveys or informal check-ins.
- Incident reporting: Log any incidents or issues reported by employees.

DATA MONITORING

- Review metrics: Check daily HR metrics dashboards for any anomalies.
- Respond to queries: Address employee questions or concerns related to policies or incidents.

Weekly Activities

DATA ANALYSIS

- Analyze trends: Review weekly trends in attendance, performance, and engagement data.
- Check compliance: Ensure all HR activities comply with company policies and legal requirements.

EMPLOYEE ENGAGEMENT

- Team meetings: Conduct weekly team meetings to discuss HR data and any emerging issues.
- Follow-up: Follow up on any incidents reported during the week.

MANAGER COACHING

- Weekly check-ins: Have check-ins with managers to discuss compliance with in-office work policies and other HR guidelines.

Monthly Activities

COMPREHENSIVE REVIEW

- Metrics review: Conduct a thorough review of monthly HR metrics such as turnover rates, engagement scores, and productivity.
- Employee investigations: Review any ongoing investigations for updates and resolutions.

TRAINING AND DEVELOPMENT

- Conduct training: Organize monthly training sessions on HR best practices and evidence-based decision-making.
- Support managers: Provide additional coaching to managers on enforcing policies consistently.

POLICY COMPLIANCE

- Audit practices: Perform a monthly audit to ensure all HR practices align with company policies and legal standards.

Quarterly Activities

STRATEGIC PLANNING

- Review goals: Assess the progress of HR initiatives against quarterly goals.

- Adjust strategies: Adjust HR strategies based on quarterly data insights and feedback.

EMPLOYEE INVESTIGATIONS

- Audit investigations: Conduct an audit of all investigations to ensure thoroughness and compliance.
- Report findings: Prepare a quarterly report on investigation outcomes and trends.

MANAGER DEVELOPMENT

- Training programs: Implement quarterly training programs for managers on leadership and policy enforcement.

DATA PRESENTATION

- Update leadership: Present quarterly HR data and investigation summaries to senior leadership.

Annual Activities

ANNUAL REPORT

- Compile data: Prepare an annual report summarizing HR metrics, investigation outcomes, and overall performance.
- Review policies: Conduct a comprehensive review of HR policies and update as necessary.

STRATEGIC REVIEW

- Evaluate strategy: Assess the effectiveness of HR strategies and initiatives over the past year.
- Set objectives: Set new HR objectives and strategies for the upcoming year.

COMPLIANCE AUDIT

- Conduct audit: Perform an annual audit to ensure all HR practices and investigations comply with legal and regulatory standards.

EMPLOYEE SURVEY

- Engagement survey: Conduct a comprehensive employee engagement survey to gather insights and inform future HR strategies.

PROFESSIONAL DEVELOPMENT

- Certifications and training: Encourage HR staff to pursue relevant certifications and training programs.

This checklist provides a structured approach to maintaining evidence-based HR practices and conducting thorough investigations. By consistently following these daily, weekly, monthly, quarterly, and annual activities, you can ensure your HR decisions are data-driven and aligned with organizational goals.

> I encourage you to integrate this checklist into your routine to enhance the effectiveness of your HR practices and investigations. By doing so, you will strengthen your strategic impact and contribute to the overall success of your organization.

Thinking Analytically: Reflections to Propel HR Forward

Data is an essential asset for HR professionals looking to make informed, strategic decisions. It's not just about gathering numbers but understanding how those numbers connect to broader business goals. Whether we are working on compensation surveys or DEIB initiatives, as HR leaders, we must ask ourselves how effectively we are utilizing data to influence decision-making. This means assessing whether the metrics we track—like turnover rates, engagement scores, or training completion—are aligned with our organization's strategic goals. If they aren't, it's time to reconsider what we're measuring.

Our decision-making should be driven by data, not intuition or anecdotal evidence. For example, when considering a shift in talent management strategies, data insights should guide our actions, ensuring that we are not simply reacting to short-term challenges but addressing underlying issues backed by evidence. This ability to integrate data into decision-making helps HR transition from being reactive to becoming proactive, solidifying its role as a strategic partner in the business.

But leveraging data effectively requires the right tools and skills. Are you equipping your team with the necessary analytics tools to process and interpret data, and are you providing them with ongoing training? Empowering your HR team to master these skills will not only make their roles more impactful but also elevate the entire department's influence within the organization.

Communication is another key area where data plays a crucial role. It's not enough to gather insights; HR leaders must effectively communicate those insights to leadership and other stakeholders. Visualizing data in an impactful, clear way ensures that it resonates with those who need to understand the bigger picture. This communication ties back to one of HR's core values: Bringing Clarity From the Clouds. We have the ability to transform complex data into actionable insights, making strategic direction easier for the entire organization to follow.

Another important factor is continuous improvement. Data analysis should not be a one-off activity but a regular part of HR's routine. Regularly review your metrics and data collection methods to ensure they remain aligned with your organization's evolving goals. Are there new data sources or tools available that could provide better insights? Be adaptable, and always seek ways to enhance the depth and quality of your data.

Benchmarking is another important step in evaluating your progress. Are your metrics on par with industry standards? If not, take a close look at where your gaps lie and how they can be addressed. Aligning your HR strategies with competitive benchmarks ensures that you stay ahead of trends and maintain your edge in attracting and retaining talent.

Finally, the long-term impact of your initiatives must be tracked and measured consistently. This is where the Forward and Adaptive Beats Static and Slow value comes into play. HR's role in driving business outcomes is constantly evolving, and our data strategies must evolve along with it. By regularly evaluating how our initiatives perform over time, we can ensure that we're not just making short-term fixes but driving long-term success for both our employees and the business.

In conclusion, data-driven decision-making is not just an operational necessity—it's a strategic imperative. By harnessing the power of analytics, HR professionals can demonstrate their value to the organization, ensure alignment with business goals, and drive impactful change. Applying the five HR values—Own Your Expertise; Be Part Coach, Part Cheerleader; Ignite the Spark; Bring Clarity From the Clouds; and Forward and Adaptive Beats Static and Slow—will help you fully leverage data in a way that advances both HR and organizational success. The future of HR lies in how well we can integrate data into every facet of our decision-making process, making us indispensable in shaping the business's future.

Conclusion

As we conclude this chapter, it's clear that HR's role as a strategic partner in the organization is inseparable from the use of data and analytics. Evidence-based decision-making is no longer optional, it's a requirement for HR leaders who want to add tangible value. By continuously collecting and analyzing data, communicating insights clearly, and aligning strategies with organizational goals, HR professionals can elevate their impact. Sophia Martinez's fictional journey is just one example of how harnessing data can lead to meaningful change. Remember, the key is not just in collecting data but in interpreting it, communicating its significance, and using it to shape the future of your workforce. By embracing the power of HR analytics, you'll be better equipped to meet the challenges of today's evolving business landscape, ensuring that HR remains at the forefront of driving organizational success.

Reference

Oracle and the HR Research Institute (2021) The State of HR Analytics 2021, Oracle, www.oracle.com/a/ocom/docs/applications/human-capital-management/hrt-talent-analytics-hrdotcom.pdf (archived at https://perma.cc/X7ZD-4DK6)

5

Aligning Strategy and Effective Communication

Introduction

In today's rapidly evolving business landscape, the role of HR is not just about managing people—it's about strategically aligning the workforce with the organization's goals to drive success. As businesses face unprecedented challenges, from technological advancements to shifting workforce dynamics, HR must take on a consultative role, thinking like a strategic partner rather than an administrative function.

This chapter emphasizes the importance of HR's ability to not only craft effective solutions but also communicate the value of those solutions to stakeholders along the value chain. By thinking like a consultant and acting like an owner, HR leaders can make informed, data-driven decisions that benefit both the business and its people. This chapter provides valuable insights into how to adopt this mindset while showcasing real-world examples of how aligning HR with organizational goals creates lasting impact.

To get started, let's hear about Marco Silva, a Talent Acquisition Director at a fictional hotel business. Marco faces a significant challenge: poor reviews and a tarnished employer brand that deter potential hires. This story highlights how Marco transformed the hotel's reputation by aligning HR strategies with business goals, improving service quality, and crafting a compelling employer brand, ultimately driving organizational success.

Strategic Synergies: Aligning HR and Business Goals

In the vibrant and competitive hospitality scene of Miami, Florida, Ocean Breeze Resort was struggling to make its mark. The hotel, known for its prime location and picturesque views, was plagued by low reviews on booking websites, impacting both customer experience and employee morale. At the center of this storm was Marco Silva, the Talent Acquisition Director, tasked with attracting the right talent to elevate the hotel's reputation and performance.

Marco sat in his office, the hum of Miami's bustling streets below, pondering his dilemma. Despite his best efforts, the hotel's ratings on popular booking websites remained low, and to make matters worse, employer branding websites painted an unsatisfactory picture of the CEO's leadership. These negative reviews were deterring potential talent, making it even harder for Marco to fill key positions.

Desperate for a solution, Marco reached out to me for some strategic guidance. We connected over a video call, and I listened as Marco shared his challenges. I knew that to turn this challenge into an opportunity, Marco needed to align the hotel's talent acquisition strategy with its business goals and create a compelling employer brand.

I began, "The first step is to understand the root causes of these negative reviews. Gather feedback from employees and guests to identify the key issues. Once you have this data, you can develop a targeted strategy to address them."

Taking this advice, Marco conducted comprehensive surveys among the staff and guests. The feedback revealed several areas needing improvement, such as inconsistent service quality, lack of employee engagement, and poor leadership communication. Armed with this information, Marco set out to transform the hotel's reputation from the inside out.

Marco knew that a strong employer brand was crucial for attracting top talent. He collaborated with the marketing team to revamp the hotel's online presence, showcasing the positive aspects of working at Ocean Breeze Resort. They created engaging content highlighting employee stories, career development opportunities, and the hotel's commitment to a supportive work environment.

Additionally, Marco organized workshops and training sessions to improve service quality and employee engagement. He worked closely with department heads to implement regular feedback loops, ensuring that employees felt heard and valued. To address the leadership issues, Marco encouraged the CEO to participate in these initiatives, demonstrating a commitment to change and transparency.

Marco also partnered with local hospitality schools and universities to create internship programs, providing students with hands-on experience at the hotel. These programs not only helped fill staffing gaps but also served as a pipeline for future talent.

As the new strategies took root, the atmosphere at Ocean Breeze Resort began to shift. Employees felt more engaged and motivated, leading to improved service quality and happier guests. Positive reviews started to trickle in, slowly but surely lifting the hotel's ratings on booking websites.

To measure the impact of his initiatives, Marco implemented a robust tracking system, monitoring key metrics such as employee turnover, guest satisfaction scores, and recruitment success rates. The data showed a significant improvement in all areas, validating the effectiveness of his strategy.

Eighteen months later, Marco presented his findings to the leadership team. "By aligning our talent acquisition strategy with our business goals and focusing on creating a positive employer brand, we've turned our challenges into opportunities," he explained. "Our improved service quality has not only enhanced the guest experience but also boosted our reputation as an employer of choice."

Marco's strategic approach had successfully transformed Ocean Breeze Resort's fortunes. His story underscored a vital lesson: effective communication and alignment between HR and business goals are essential for driving organizational success. By addressing the root causes of issues and creating a compelling employer brand, HR can play a pivotal role in turning challenges into opportunities.

Reflecting on his journey, Marco felt a deep sense of pride. He had not only attracted the right talent but had also contributed to the hotel's overall success. His story, like many others in this book, highlights the power of strategic synergies in aligning HR and business goals for lasting impact.

Communicating Value: HR's Role in Strategic Execution

In today's business environment, it is crucial that HR not only supports but also drives strategic initiatives. By effectively communicating our value, we can ensure that HR is recognized as a critical partner in achieving organizational goals.

Every senior HR professional must be able to articulate the value of your contributions to the organization. It's not enough to implement HR initiatives; we must also demonstrate how these initiatives align with and support the organization's strategic objectives. And to take matters further, we must be persuasive and influential to ensure buy-in from all relevant stakeholders. Let's dive into how we can effectively communicate the value of HR in strategic execution.

Understanding HR's Strategic Role

HR AS A STRATEGIC PARTNER

HR's role extends far beyond traditional administrative functions. We are strategic partners who influence key business decisions and drive organizational success. Our responsibilities include talent management, employee engagement, leadership development, and culture shaping—each of which is crucial for executing the company's strategy. For example, a well-designed talent management strategy ensures that the organization has the right people in the right roles, directly impacting business performance.

ALIGNING HR INITIATIVES WITH BUSINESS GOALS

To communicate our value, we must first ensure that our HR initiatives are aligned with the broader business goals. This involves understanding the company's strategic objectives and developing HR strategies that support these goals. For instance, if a company's goal is to innovate, HR can contribute by fostering a culture of creativity and continuous learning. By aligning our initiatives with business objectives, we can clearly demonstrate how HR contributes to achieving these goals.

Communicating Value Effectively

USING DATA AND METRICS

One of the most powerful ways to communicate HR's value is through data and metrics. By tracking and reporting key performance indicators, we can provide tangible evidence of our impact. For example, metrics such as employee turnover rates, engagement scores, and time-to-fill for key positions can highlight the effectiveness of our HR initiatives. Presenting this data in a clear and compelling manner helps stakeholders understand the value we bring to the organization.

STORYTELLING WITH DATA

While data is important, it's equally crucial to tell a compelling story. Combining data with real-life examples and narratives makes the information more relatable and impactful. For example, if we've implemented a new leadership development program, we can share success stories of employees who have benefited from the program and how their development has positively impacted the organization. This approach helps to humanize the data and connect it to the broader organizational goals.

ENGAGING STAKEHOLDERS

Engaging stakeholders at all levels is essential for communicating HR's value. This means regularly updating senior leadership on HR initiatives and their impact, as well as communicating with managers and employees. Regular town hall meetings, detailed reports, and interactive dashboards are effective tools for this. For instance, a quarterly HR report that highlights key achievements, challenges, and plans for the future can keep stakeholders informed and engaged.

Practical Strategies for Communicating Value

REGULAR REPORTING

Implementing a structured reporting system is crucial. Regularly share HR metrics and insights with senior leadership. This could be through monthly or quarterly reports that track progress against strategic goals. For example, if one of the goals is to reduce turnover, the report should include current turnover rates, comparison with industry benchmarks, and actions being taken to address the issue.

LEADERSHIP BRIEFINGS

Hold regular briefings with senior leadership to discuss HR's strategic contributions. These meetings should focus on how HR initiatives are driving business success and what plans are in place to continue this trajectory. For example, a briefing might cover the impact of a new performance management system on employee productivity and morale.

EMPLOYEE FEEDBACK

Collecting and sharing employee feedback can also demonstrate HR's value. Regularly conduct surveys and share the results with the broader organization, highlighting areas of improvement and actions taken. For instance, after implementing a new employee wellness program, sharing feedback from employees about its positive impact can illustrate the program's value.

In summary, effectively communicating the value of HR in strategic execution involves aligning HR initiatives with business goals, using data and metrics to demonstrate impact, telling compelling stories, and engaging stakeholders through regular reporting and briefings.

I encourage you to take these strategies back to your organization and implement them. By doing so, you can ensure that your HR department is recognized as a critical driver of strategic success and that your contributions are clearly understood and valued.

Mentor's Corner: Strategic Alignment as a Consultative Thought Partner

When you think like a consultant and act like an owner as an HR leader, you're not just solving problems—you're guiding your organization toward long-term success. It's not about handling challenges reactively but proactively seeking out root causes and addressing them in a systematic, informed way. Consultants have a unique mindset: they approach problems by gathering information, evaluating possible solutions, and implementing the best practices they've encountered in their experience. As an HR leader, whether you work within an organization or as an external advisor, this way of thinking is crucial. When you adopt a consultant's lens, you remain impartial, analytical, and strategic.

At the same time, acting like an owner brings in a whole new dimension. It's not just about solving a problem—it's about owning it. You take responsibility for the outcome as if the success of the entire business depends on it. When you combine these two approaches, you gain the strategic foresight of a consultant with the dedication and commitment of an owner, making you an invaluable asset to your organization. The ability to think long-term, to take personal responsibility for decisions, and to ensure that your solutions align with the company's overarching goals is essential for any HR leader.

The Consultant Mindset

Thinking like a consultant means breaking problems down into manageable parts and using data, experience, and best practices to find solutions. The goal is to bring structure to what can often be a chaotic situation. For example, if employee engagement is low, the consultant approach isn't to simply run an engagement survey and implement surface-level solutions. Instead, you'd dig deeper. What are the real causes of disengagement? Is it leadership? Company culture? Poor communication? The consultant asks these questions to ensure the root cause is identified, rather than focusing solely on the symptoms.

This mindset is especially important because HR leaders deal with multiple stakeholders—senior executives, board members, employees, prospective staff, community partners, and vendors. Each of these groups has its own goals, concerns, and perspectives. The best HR leaders know how to take all of these viewpoints into consideration, much like a consultant does when dealing with multiple clients. They must bridge gaps, find common ground, and present solutions that address the needs of the entire organization.

An example might be in managing a merger or acquisition. The HR leader needs to understand the strategic goals of the company and the fears or concerns of employees. The ability to think like a consultant helps you provide a roadmap that brings all stakeholders into alignment while navigating the complexities of change.

I can think of a time in my career where I was brought in to a media technology company in New York City to provide stability to the HR function. One of the many challenges the company faced was a lease that was expiring in a couple of months. The owner, who lived in Connecticut, no longer wanted the long train ride into the office and thought it would be best if the company moved to Connecticut where office space is cheaper. While it is important to think about the ability to save money, there was one major problem: Many of the employees lived in New Jersey and the commute to and from Connecticut would have tripled or quadrupled their commute. This was a situation where I was tasked with finding a winning solution under serious time constraints.

In order to give the owner of the business a clear picture of the status of his workforce, I put together a list of all of the addresses of the employees, color coded by seniority, and the drive time, cost of tolls, and time of commute for employees who would be asked to commute by public transportation or car into another state. Once the owner saw how the move would have impacted his staff, we decided on a better solution—moving the entire staff to a coworking facility in mid-town Manhattan that sat right above the train he took every day into the office. Did he shave off time from his daily commute? Barely. Did he preserve his workforce and continue to grow? Yes he did! Whether you are internal or external HR, be ready to solve problems in a way where the greatest good to the organization is achieved.

Acting Like an Owner

While thinking like a consultant is critical for problem-solving, acting like an owner ensures you are committed to seeing your solutions through. Owners care deeply about the outcomes—they aren't just focused on getting the job done but making sure it's done well and with lasting positive impact. Acting like an owner also means being willing to take on responsibility for the outcome, no matter who ultimately gets the credit.

One of the biggest challenges HR leaders face is navigating tension between different stakeholders. For instance, senior executives may want to cut costs while employees are pushing for higher wages. Acting like an owner means that you care deeply about the wellbeing of employees while also understanding the financial pressures the company faces. You don't just act as a mediator—you take ownership of finding a solution that serves both parties. By treating the organization's challenges as your own, you can move from simply being a neutral party to becoming a key driver of progress.

This is also where HR leaders stand out. The ability to manage tension and deliver results is what separates good HR leaders from great ones. Whether it's negotiating new policies with employees or working with vendors to create better benefit programs, owning the outcome ensures your focus remains on creating win-win solutions that push the company forward.

Let me tell you about a time where an owner's mindset went a long way in conflict and crisis resolution. In the early days of running my practice, Jumpstart HR, we supported a religious nonprofit that was a major organization in the community. The organization ran a weekly food pantry for those in need, sent students on life-changing missions overseas, and drew thousands of congregation members a week to its religious services on weekends. Prior to my firm supporting it, the nonprofit relied on volunteers to handle the HR function and it left a few operational holes unfilled.

One of those holes was staff sentiment that they were underpaid. There started to be an uptick in turnover and most exit surveys pointed to compensation as a factor for leaving the organization. So what did we do? Not only did Jumpstart HR conduct compensation analysis to determine whether staff members were fairly compensated, we also started the practice of giving employees their annual total compensation report at the end of the year. The leadership team of the organization knew that their growth and prosperity had much to do with the team that worked tirelessly on behalf of the community. And continuing to lose talented employees was no longer acceptable.

By presenting staff with a clear picture of their compensation in comparison with organizations of the same size and industry, it gave a clear perspective that their worth was respected by management. By sharing total compensation figures with individuals, we were able to show that there were more dollars and cents invested on their behalf in the form of 100 percent employer-paid health insurance premiums, generous paid time off, employer-provided life and disability insurance, and other perks. This was a time where acting like an owner showed management that we are committed to creative problem-solving and showed staff members that we can be trusted to advocate for their best interests.

Operating as a Diplomat

The best HR leaders often act like diplomats—bridging gaps between opposing stakeholders, finding common ground, and helping both sides move forward together. This requires an ability to navigate conflict with empathy and skill. As an HR leader, you are constantly tasked with balancing the needs of the business with the concerns of employees. Diplomacy is key in this balancing act. Whether you're negotiating terms for a new employment policy, resolving conflicts between teams, or advocating for organizational change, the ability to remain impartial yet influential makes all the difference.

You can't simply take sides. Instead, you listen to both groups, understand their needs, and guide them toward a solution that benefits everyone involved. This is especially crucial when dealing with sensitive topics like layoffs, restructuring, or cultural shifts. The best HR leaders know how to present a clear vision that addresses these difficult situations while maintaining trust and morale within the company.

Sometimes that is easier said than done, and I understand that personally. There was a time when I had been tasked with helping a minority-serving institution improve morale in the midst of serious budgetary chaos. Managers were pulling for the organization to be run exactly how they wanted it to be run. Employees were pushing for their voices to be heard because they'd felt for so long that their suggestions were falling on deaf ears. Sometimes you as an HR leader will carry the intimate details and trust of both perspectives, and it can be heavy! My hope is that you have people to reach out to for mentorship and that you apply the five HR values to reclaim your peace, power, and success!

Applying the Five HR Values

Now, let's explore how the five HR values align with the approach of thinking like a consultant and acting like an owner.

OWN YOUR EXPERTISE

Owning your expertise means knowing that your HR experience is invaluable when addressing complex issues. When you think like a consultant, you rely on your expertise to guide the process and make decisions based on best practices. You own the role of expert in the room, helping others understand the reasoning behind your decisions, which fosters trust and respect.

BE PART COACH, PART CHEERLEADER

Acting as both a coach and a cheerleader ties directly into thinking like a consultant and acting like an owner. As a coach, you guide stakeholders through changes, help them understand the implications of decisions, and support their development. As a cheerleader, you motivate the team, rally support for HR initiatives, and maintain a positive outlook even in challenging situations.

IGNITE THE SPARK

HR's ability to ignite the spark comes from understanding what drives both the business and its people. Thinking like a consultant allows you to see opportunities where others might see obstacles. Whether it's redesigning an outdated performance management system or spearheading a new engagement strategy, HR leaders ignite change by finding innovative solutions that align with business goals.

BRING CLARITY FROM THE CLOUDS

Thinking like a consultant helps you bring clarity to complex issues. In HR, it's common to deal with ambiguity—whether it's in managing workforce planning or navigating employee relations issues. Acting like an owner means taking these abstract challenges and breaking them down into actionable steps that everyone can understand. Clarity is essential when leading any initiative.

FORWARD AND ADAPTIVE BEATS STATIC AND SLOW

The ability to think like a consultant encourages adaptability. Consultants are always forward-thinking, planning for what's next. HR leaders must be just as adaptive, ready to pivot as organizational priorities shift. Acting like an owner reinforces the urgency of staying ahead of the curve, ensuring that HR remains agile in addressing the company's evolving needs.

Conclusion

In today's business environment, HR leaders must think like consultants and act like owners. This dual approach allows you to bring structured problem-solving to the table while demonstrating a deep commitment to the success of the organization. You're not just an administrator—you're a strategic partner with the power to influence, lead, and drive change. By applying the five HR values—Own Your Expertise; Be Part Coach, Part Cheerleader; Ignite the Spark;

Bring Clarity From the Clouds; and Forward and Adaptive Beats Static and Slow—you can elevate your role and make a lasting impact on your company. Whether you're managing stakeholder tensions, driving business goals, or navigating change, thinking like a consultant and acting like an owner ensures your HR leadership is both influential and essential.

Communication Breakdowns: Lessons from the Field

Effective communication is the backbone of any successful organization, and understanding how to navigate and rectify breakdowns is crucial for HR leaders. And communication breakdowns are a big deal at work. According to a 2023 Forbes.com article, 45 percent of workers suffer from lost trust at work due to poor communication (Hoory, 2023). The shift to remote and hybrid workforces has only made communication more difficult.

As senior HR professionals, our role includes ensuring clear and effective communication across all levels of the organization. When communication fails, it can lead to misunderstandings, decreased morale, and ultimately a negative impact on business performance. Let's delve into some lessons from the field that highlight the importance of effective communication and how to address breakdowns when they occur.

Understanding Communication Breakdowns

CAUSES OF COMMUNICATION BREAKDOWNS
Communication breakdowns can occur for various reasons, including unclear messaging, lack of transparency, and cultural differences. For example, in a company undergoing rapid growth, unclear communication about new processes and roles can lead to confusion and frustration among employees. Similarly, a lack of transparency during a company restructuring can create anxiety and rumors, further exacerbating the situation.

IMPACT ON ORGANIZATIONS

The impact of communication breakdowns can be significant. They can lead to decreased employee engagement, lower productivity, and increased turnover. For instance, if employees feel they are not being heard or kept in the loop about important changes, their trust in leadership can erode. This can result in disengagement and a lack of commitment to the organization's goals.

Lessons from the Field

MISHAP #1: THE MERGER MISHAP

In one notable case, a media technology firm that worked with my company experienced a significant communication breakdown during a merger. The leadership team failed to clearly communicate the reasons behind the merger and how it would benefit the employees. As a result, there was widespread uncertainty and resistance, leading to a drop in productivity and a spike in employee turnover. The lesson here is the importance of clear, transparent communication, especially during significant organizational changes. Employees need to understand the "why" behind decisions to feel secure and engaged.

MISHAP #2: THE TECH ROLLOUT FAILURE

Another example comes from a technology company that rolled out a new recruitment platform without adequately training employees or explaining its benefits. The lack of proper communication led to low adoption rates and frustration among employees who found the new system cumbersome. Jumpstart HR was brought in to train employees on the new system and to turn on all features that were being paid for but underutilized. This case underscores the importance of not only communicating the introduction of new tools but also providing the necessary training and support to ensure smooth adoption. Employees should feel confident in their ability to use new systems and understand how these tools will improve their work processes.

MISHAP #3: THE REMOTE WORK CHALLENGE

During the Covid-19 pandemic, many organizations faced challenges with the sudden shift to remote work. One nonprofit client struggled with maintaining effective communication as employees transitioned from working together in Washington, DC to working from home. The initial lack of structured communication channels led to feelings of isolation and disconnection among team members. By establishing regular virtual check-ins, clear guidelines, and open channels for feedback, the company eventually improved communication and morale. This example highlights the importance of adapting communication strategies to fit new working conditions and ensuring that employees remain connected and informed.

Strategies for Addressing Communication Breakdowns

ESTABLISH CLEAR CHANNELS

To prevent communication breakdowns, it is essential to establish clear and consistent communication channels. This includes regular updates from leadership, structured team meetings, and accessible platforms for information sharing. For example, implementing a weekly company-wide newsletter can keep employees informed about important updates and changes.

ENCOURAGE FEEDBACK

Encouraging open feedback from employees is crucial for identifying and addressing communication issues. Regular surveys, suggestion boxes, and town hall meetings can provide valuable insights into areas where communication may be lacking. Acting on this feedback shows employees that their voices are heard and valued, fostering a culture of open communication.

PROVIDE TRAINING

Effective communication skills are not innate for everyone; they need to be developed. Providing training on communication best practices for both leaders and employees can significantly improve the quality of communication within the organization. For instance, workshops on active listening, clear messaging, and effective virtual communication can equip employees with the tools they need to communicate more effectively.

BE TRANSPARENT

Transparency from leadership is essential for building trust and preventing rumors and misinformation. This means being open about the reasons behind decisions, the expected outcomes, and the potential impacts on employees. For example, during periods of change, holding regular Q&A sessions where employees can ask questions and get direct answers from leadership can alleviate concerns and build trust.

In summary, communication breakdowns can have significant negative impacts on an organization, but they can be addressed and prevented through clear communication channels, encouraging feedback, providing training, and maintaining transparency. By learning from past mistakes and implementing these strategies, we can ensure that communication remains effective and supports organizational success.

> I encourage you to reflect on your current communication practices and identify areas for improvement. By proactively addressing potential communication breakdowns, you can create a more connected, informed, and engaged workforce.

CASE STUDY EXERCISE
Strategic Communication in Action

You are the HR Director at a small dog food manufacturing company, PupChow Inc. The company is planning a major strategic shift to focus more on artificial intelligence and machine learning technologies. This shift will involve significant changes, including re-skilling current employees, hiring new talent with specialized skills, and potentially phasing out certain legacy products. As part of this transition, effective communication will be crucial to ensure employee buy-in, reduce uncertainty, and align everyone with the new strategic direction.

Please note: This case study is entirely fictitious. Any relationship to a real-world organization or person is entirely coincidental.

Task

Develop a comprehensive communication plan to support the strategic shift at PupChow Inc. Your plan should address how to communicate the changes to different stakeholders, manage potential resistance, and ensure ongoing engagement throughout the transition.

Supporting Questions

- Who are the key stakeholders affected by the strategic shift to AI and ML technologies?
- What are the core messages that need to be communicated about the strategic shift?
- What communication channels will be most effective for reaching each stakeholder group?
- How will you keep employees engaged and informed throughout the transition?
- What metrics will you use to measure the effectiveness of your communication plan?

Strategic Alignment Checklist: Your Communication Plan

Daily Activities

MONITOR COMMUNICATION CHANNELS

- Check emails and messages: Respond promptly to important communications.
- Engage with employees: Have informal conversations to gauge employee sentiment and gather feedback.

TRACK PROGRESS

- Update task lists: Review and update your daily task list to stay on track with communication goals.
- Monitor KPIs: Keep an eye on key performance indicators relevant to HR communications.

Weekly Activities

TEAM MEETINGS

- Hold weekly HR team meetings: Discuss ongoing projects, share updates, and align on communication strategies.
- Engage with other departments: Attend cross-functional meetings to stay informed about their needs and how HR can support them.

REVIEW METRICS

- Analyze communication effectiveness: Review metrics such as open rates for emails, participation in meetings, and feedback received.
- Adjust strategies: Make necessary adjustments to communication plans based on weekly insights.

STAKEHOLDER CHECK-INS

- Regular check-ins: Have check-ins with key stakeholders to discuss ongoing initiatives and gather feedback.

Monthly Activities

COMPREHENSIVE REVIEW

- Evaluate HR initiatives: Conduct a monthly review of HR initiatives and their alignment with strategic goals.
- Assess communication channels: Evaluate the effectiveness of communication channels and make improvements as needed.

EMPLOYEE FEEDBACK

- Conduct surveys: Send out monthly surveys to gather employee feedback on recent communications and initiatives.
- Analyze feedback: Review survey results and identify areas for improvement.

CONTENT PLANNING

- Plan monthly communications: Develop a content calendar for the upcoming month, including key messages, events, and updates.
- Prepare materials: Create and review communication materials to ensure clarity and alignment with strategic goals.

Quarterly activities

STRATEGIC ALIGNMENT

- Review strategic goals: Assess the alignment of HR initiatives with the organization's quarterly goals.
- Adjust plans: Update communication strategies to ensure they support the latest business objectives.

STAKEHOLDER REPORTS

- Prepare reports: Compile quarterly reports on HR initiatives and their impact, including key metrics and success stories.
- Present findings: Share these reports with senior leadership and other stakeholders.

TRAINING AND DEVELOPMENT

- Conduct training: Offer quarterly training sessions on communication best practices for HR staff and managers.
- Review skills: Assess the communication skills of your team and identify areas for development.

EMPLOYEE ENGAGEMENT

- Engagement activities: Plan and execute quarterly employee engagement activities to foster a positive organizational culture.

Annual Activities

ANNUAL REPORT

- Compile data: Prepare an annual report summarizing HR initiatives, communication efforts, and their impact on strategic goals.
- Review outcomes: Evaluate the overall success of your communication strategies over the past year.

STRATEGIC PLANNING

- Set goals: Develop communication goals and strategies for the upcoming year, aligned with the organization's strategic objectives.
- Budget planning: Allocate resources and budget for communication initiatives.

POLICY REVIEW

- Review policies: Conduct an annual review of communication policies and procedures to ensure they are up-to-date and effective.
- Update policies: Make necessary updates to reflect changes in organizational priorities or best practices.

EMPLOYEE SURVEY

- Conduct comprehensive survey: Execute an annual employee engagement survey to gather in-depth feedback.
- Analyze and act: Review the results and develop action plans to address any identified issues.

- Invest in training: Identify and pursue opportunities for professional development in communication for HR staff.

- Certifications and courses: Encourage team members to complete relevant certifications and courses.

This structured checklist ensures that HR leaders consistently engage in activities that enhance communication, align HR initiatives with business goals, and demonstrate strategic value. By breaking down actions into daily, weekly, monthly, quarterly, and annual tasks, we can maintain focus, drive continuous improvement, and enhance our impact.

> I encourage each of you to integrate this checklist into your routine to enhance the effectiveness of your HR communication practices. By consistently following these actions, you can showcase HR's contributions and drive organizational success.

Reflective Insights: Are You Truly Aligned?

When it comes to aligning HR initiatives with the broader goals of an organization, the role of HR is more crucial than ever. It's not enough for HR to operate in isolation, focusing on traditional tasks like recruitment and benefits. HR must act as a strategic partner that understands and actively supports the company's long-term objectives. A key question every HR leader should ask themselves is: How well do our current HR initiatives align with the overall strategic goals of the organization? If there are gaps, then it's critical to identify where improvements can be made and take proactive steps to bridge those gaps.

Understanding the organization's business objectives, both short-term and long-term, is fundamental. You can't align HR initiatives with company goals if you're not clear on what those goals are. Make it a point to stay informed about changes in strategic direction. This means building strong relationships with leadership and ensuring that you're part of the strategic conversations from the outset. HR's strategic role is to drive talent acquisition, development, and engagement in a way that directly supports business objectives, whether that's growing revenue, expanding into new markets, or improving operational efficiency.

Communication is another critical piece. It's one thing to understand the strategic goals, but quite another to ensure that the entire HR team—and the wider organization—knows how HR initiatives align with those goals. Bring clarity from the clouds by effectively communicating how HR strategies directly support the overall business strategy. Use multiple channels—team meetings, one-on-one conversations, and company-wide communications—to keep everyone informed and aligned.

Feedback and collaboration are essential for ensuring that HR initiatives are not only aligned with strategic goals but also adapted as those goals evolve. Collaborating with other departments allows HR to gain insights into how well initiatives are working and where adjustments may be needed. Building these partnerships ensures HR is seen as a forward and adaptive department, capable of influencing company strategy.

Measuring impact is where HR can truly demonstrate its value. Tracking the success of HR initiatives through key performance indicators such as employee engagement, retention, and performance metrics shows how HR is contributing to the company's goals. Regularly reviewing these metrics and making necessary adjustments to strategies ensures ongoing alignment. Own your expertise by developing a deep understanding of how to measure HR's contribution to organizational success and presenting those metrics in a way that leadership understands.

Finally, being part coach, part cheerleader is about empowering your team and the organization at large to embrace the cultural changes necessary to meet strategic goals. HR initiatives, when properly aligned, are not just about ticking boxes—they're about fostering a strong organizational culture that supports growth, innovation, and engagement. It's your responsibility as an HR leader to drive these cultural shifts, ensuring that employees feel connected to the company's mission and vision.

In summary, the power of HR lies in its ability to influence, align, and drive organizational success. By understanding business goals, maintaining open communication, collaborating across departments, measuring impact, and continuously adapting, HR can ensure it remains a key strategic partner in the company's success.

> Regularly reflecting on these questions can help you identify strengths and areas for improvement in aligning HR strategies with organizational goals. Use these insights to drive more effective and impactful HR practices.

Conclusion

As HR professionals, it's crucial to recognize the power we have to influence, shape, and drive organizational success. When we think like consultants and act like owners, we place ourselves in a position of influence, where we can bridge gaps, solve complex problems, and align our work with the company's strategic goals. This chapter has shown how communication, collaboration, and strategic thinking can elevate HR's role from a support function to a key driver of business success. By embracing the five HR values—Own Your Expertise; Be Part Coach, Part Cheerleader; Ignite the Spark; Bring Clarity From the Clouds; and Forward and Adaptive Beats Static and Slow—we ensure that HR remains at the forefront of organizational progress, delivering results that matter and ensuring that both the business and its people thrive. Now is the time to take these lessons forward and apply them in your day-to-day work, leading with confidence and strategic clarity.

Reference

Hoory, L (2023) The State of Workplace Communication in 2023—Forbes Advisor, Forbes, www.forbes.com/advisor/business/digital-communication-workplace/ (archived at https://perma.cc/7M6Q-BAND)

PART 2

A Blueprint for HR's Unique Impact

6

Talent Management

Introduction

This is the chapter where I am excited to discuss a fundamental aspect of HR that lies at the heart of organizational success: talent management. Managing talent effectively is not just about filling positions; it's about nurturing and developing the potential within our workforce to drive long-term success. This process is pivotal for creating a competitive edge and ensuring that your organization thrives in a rapidly changing business environment.

In this fictional example that opens this chapter, an email from a CEO to her HR Director highlights the transformative power of strategic talent management. Facing financial crisis, strategic HR initiatives in retention, workforce planning, and continuous learning saved the company. This chapter illustrates how forward-thinking talent management can be essential in overcoming challenges and driving organizational success.

Talent Triumphs: Stories of Strategic Talent Management

Subject: Celebrating Our Talent Management Success
Dear Samantha,

I hope this email finds you well. As we reflect on the past year, I wanted to take a moment to personally acknowledge the monumental impact your efforts in talent management have had on our organization. When we were facing the looming threat of insolvency, your strategic initiatives not only helped us overcome this monstrous challenge but also positioned us for a brighter future.

There are three key aspects of your talent management strategy that I believe were instrumental in saving our organization.

1. Developing a comprehensive talent retention program

Your foresight in identifying and addressing the root causes of our high turnover rates was crucial. By implementing a comprehensive talent retention program that included competitive compensation packages, career development opportunities, and a robust employee recognition system, we were able to retain our top performers and maintain continuity in our operations. This stability was essential in navigating the financial turmoil and ensuring we had the right people in place to drive our recovery efforts.

2. Implementing data-driven workforce planning

Your use of data analytics to inform our workforce planning decisions was a game-changer. By accurately predicting future staffing needs and identifying skills gaps, you enabled us to make proactive hiring decisions and optimize our talent allocation. This not only improved our operational efficiency but also reduced unnecessary labor costs, contributing significantly to our financial turnaround. The ability to align our workforce strategy with our business goals provided us with a strategic advantage that was critical in our fight against insolvency.

3. Fostering a culture of continuous improvement and learning

Your commitment to fostering a culture of continuous improvement and learning has had a profound impact on our organizational resilience. The training programs and professional development opportunities you introduced empowered our employees to upskill and adapt to the changing business environment. This adaptability was vital in our ability to pivot and innovate during challenging times. Moreover, the emphasis on lifelong learning has created a motivated and engaged workforce that is now better equipped to drive our future success.

Samantha, your leadership in talent management has been nothing short of transformative. The initiatives you championed not only helped us avert a financial disaster but also laid the foundation for a sustainable and prosperous future. I firmly believe that without your strategic vision and tireless efforts, we would not have survived this critical period.

As we move forward, I am confident that your continued focus on strategic talent management will remain a cornerstone of our success. Thank you for your unwavering dedication and for being the driving force behind our triumph over adversity.

With deepest appreciation,

Marsha Brown,

CEO

Managing to Succeed:
The Cornerstone of Effective Talent Management

As senior HR leaders, we play a critical role in shaping the talent strategies that align with our business objectives. Our ability to manage talent effectively directly impacts employee engagement, productivity, and retention. By focusing on strategic talent management, we can ensure that our organization has the right people in the right roles, equipped with the skills they need to succeed.

Understanding Effective Talent Management

The Strategic Importance

Effective talent management begins with understanding its strategic importance. It's about aligning talent strategies with the overall business goals to drive performance and growth. For example, if your organization's goal is to innovate, your talent management strategy should focus on attracting and developing creative thinkers and problem solvers. By linking talent management to business outcomes, you can demonstrate the value HR brings to the table.

Components of Talent Management

Talent management is a multifaceted process that includes attracting, developing, retaining, and optimizing talent. Each component plays a crucial role in building a robust workforce:

- **Attracting talent:** Developing a strong employer brand and effective recruitment strategies to attract top talent.
- **Developing talent:** Implementing continuous learning and development programs to enhance skills and career growth.
- **Retaining talent:** Fostering a positive work environment and offering competitive compensation and benefits to retain high performers.
- **Optimizing talent:** Ensuring that employees are in roles where they can excel and contribute to the organization's goals.

Best Practices for Talent Management

ALIGNING WITH BUSINESS GOALS

To manage talent effectively, we must align our talent management strategies with the organization's business goals. This requires a deep understanding of the business and its strategic direction. Regularly collaborating with business leaders to understand their needs and challenges allows us to tailor our talent strategies accordingly. For instance, if the company is expanding into new markets, we need to identify and develop the skills required for success in those regions.

USING DATA AND ANALYTICS

Leveraging data and analytics is essential for informed decision-making in talent management. By analyzing workforce data, we can identify trends, predict future needs, and measure the effectiveness of our talent initiatives. For example, using predictive analytics can help us anticipate turnover risks and proactively address them. Regularly reviewing key metrics such as employee engagement scores, turnover rates, and performance data enables us to refine our strategies and ensure they are impactful.

FOSTERING A CULTURE OF CONTINUOUS IMPROVEMENT

A culture of continuous improvement is vital for effective talent management. This means creating an environment where employees are encouraged to develop their skills and pursue career growth. Providing opportunities for training, mentorship, and professional development not only enhances individual performance but also drives organizational success. For instance, implementing a robust learning and development program can help employees stay current with industry trends and best practices, making our workforce more agile and competitive.

Implementing Talent Management Programs

STRUCTURED ONBOARDING

A structured onboarding program is crucial for setting new hires up for success. This includes not only orientation but also ongoing support and training. Effective onboarding helps new employees integrate into the company culture, understand their roles, and start contributing quickly. For example, a comprehensive onboarding plan that includes regular check-ins, training sessions, and mentoring can significantly improve new hire retention and productivity.

PERFORMANCE MANAGEMENT

An effective performance management system is essential for ongoing talent development. This involves setting clear expectations, providing regular feedback, and conducting performance reviews. A transparent and fair performance management process ensures that employees understand their goals and how their work contributes to the organization's success. For instance, implementing a continuous feedback system where managers provide real-time feedback can enhance employee performance and engagement.

CAREER DEVELOPMENT

Investing in career development is a key component of talent management. Providing employees with clear career paths and opportunities for advancement fosters loyalty and motivation. Offering programs such as leadership development, succession planning, and skills training can help employees achieve their career goals while aligning their growth with the organization's needs. For example, a leadership development program that identifies high-potential employees and prepares them for future leadership roles ensures a strong leadership pipeline.

In summary, managing to succeed in talent management involves aligning our strategies with business goals, using data to inform our decisions, fostering a culture of continuous improvement, and implementing effective programs for onboarding, performance management, and career development. By focusing on these areas, we can ensure that our organization not only attracts but also develops and retains top talent.

I encourage each of you to reflect on your current talent management practices and identify areas for improvement. By continuously refining our approaches and staying aligned with organizational goals, we can create a workforce that is engaged, productive, and poised for long-term success.

Mentor's Corner: How Well Do You Know Your Employees?

One of the most insightful conversations I've had in preparing to write this book came from my discussion with Julie Turney, founder and CEO of HRatHeart Consulting Inc. Julie is a leader who understands how deeply knowing your employees, their motivations, and their challenges can transform an organization. In our conversation, we focused on how HR can best demonstrate its value—not just to leadership but to every level of the company.

Creating Value for Prospective Hires

When thinking about the employee life cycle, the first thing to think about is how to showcase an organization's value to potential hires. Too often, we present a polished, superficial version of our company during recruitment processes. We might mention things like perks and benefits, but we overlook sharing what truly makes the organization unique—the aspects that a candidate wouldn't find on a website or social media page. To this effect, Julie made a powerful point: the key to standing out is to dig deeper into the company culture, especially around the aspects that matter to people. Why do employees choose to work for you and not the office across the street or the office that lets them work from the comfort of their home?

Another value that is underemphasized is just how important it is to be transparent about things like mental health support, development opportunities, and the long-term growth trajectory within the company. Candidates want to know that they will be valued as whole human beings. One such example is to not undersell the investments you make in your facilities. For example, sharing with a candidate that your company has mental health support groups or lactation rooms for new mothers shows that you care about the wellbeing of your employees, both at work and in their personal lives. This type of communication builds trust before the candidate even signs on.

We both agreed that another critical point is mapping out a career path for potential hires. This is not a new phenomenon and it is a key driver that my own research has found for why employees have left organizations for the last decade (Price, 2012). It's not enough to tell them about the position they're applying for—you must also help them visualize where that role could take them within your organization. By explaining how an entry-level accountant could rise to the position of CFO through well-defined career development frameworks, you show that you're invested in their future growth, not just filling a role. Prospective hires need to see that the organization will help them develop and thrive.

Building Trust with Non-Management Employees

From prospective hires, you must shift your focus to how HR can create value for non-management employees. Julie hit the nail on the head in stating that one of the most important things HR professionals can do is to get to know people. It's not just about knowing what job they do, but understanding who they are as individuals—what drives them, what challenges they face, and what goals they have. Building this trust helps dismantle the common misconception that HR is only there to enforce rules or fire people.

To truly support employees, HR needs to be in touch with the day-to-day realities of their work. It's about ensuring they have the tools, resources, and clarity around their objectives. Julie wants every HR leader to know that you need to make sure that your KPIs are aligned with both personal and business growth. If the goals feel irrelevant or unattainable, motivation drops and HR must intervene to bridge that gap. It's only through getting to know employees that HR can understand how to address their frustrations and help them succeed.

Supporting Mid-Level Management

Mid-level managers sit in a tricky spot. They are often the backbone of a company, managing teams, executing strategies, and ensuring smooth operations. Yet, they can feel stuck between the needs of their team and the demands of senior leadership. Julie and I agreed that HR's role with mid-level managers is twofold: support them in managing their teams while also helping them grow as leaders.

Julie says that it is important to evaluate leadership readiness before someone is placed in a management role. Too often, we promote people based on technical skills rather than leadership potential, which can lead to dysfunctional teams and timid managers. She is an advocate for understanding the true peril of "leadership risk," where unprepared managers can demotivate teams, leading to higher turnover and lower productivity. HR must play an active role in assessing a manager's capability and offering guidance through mentoring, coaching, and leadership development programs.

Julie and I also talked about psychological safety, a crucial element in keeping teams motivated and cohesive. Mid-level managers need to foster an environment where employees feel safe to share their ideas, express concerns, and take risks without fear of retaliation. HR can support managers by teaching them how to create and maintain this type of culture, ensuring long-term success for the company.

Providing Value to Senior Executives

When it comes to senior executives and the C-suite, Julie's advice was clear as well: get to know what keeps them up at night and how to resolve those challenges. As an HR professional, it's essential to understand the business, the market, and the challenges the company faces. Julie believes it is critical to have strong business acumen and to use data to present insights that are relevant to the company's strategy.

Here is where Julie leads by example. In prior organizations, she would host quarterly business reviews with C-level executives. During these meetings, they discussed not just business metrics but also the people behind the numbers. Highlighting the contributions of employees fosters recognition from the top down and ensures that executives stay connected with the team. It's also a perfect opportunity to point out potential competency gaps in leadership and provide coaching or development opportunities.

Julie stressed that HR's role with senior executives is not just about providing solutions but being proactive in bringing issues to the table, always with a proposed solution in hand. This allows HR to be seen as a strategic partner, deeply involved in the company's success.

The Five HR Values in Action

Throughout our conversation, I kept coming back to the five core HR values I've shared with you in this book. Julie's insights provided rich examples of how these values apply across various levels of the organization.

OWN YOUR EXPERTISE

Julie's emphasis on understanding the business and bringing meaningful data to the table reflects the need for HR professionals to be experts in their field. Whether it's workforce planning or leadership development, HR must confidently own their role as the expert in these areas.

BE PART COACH, PART CHEERLEADER

Coaching and supporting employees at all levels is essential, but so is celebrating their successes. Julie's point about recognizing the contributions of team members during executive meetings shows how HR can be both coach and cheerleader, boosting morale while driving performance.

IGNITE THE SPARK

HR has the power to ignite change and growth within an organization. Julie talked about fostering psychological safety and personal development, which encourages creativity and innovation among teams. By focusing on culture and wellbeing, HR can light the spark that drives mutual trust and organizational success.

BRING CLARITY FROM THE CLOUDS

Julie reminded me of the importance of providing clarity in complex situations. Whether it's setting clear KPIs for non-management employees or helping senior executives understand the talent landscape, HR's role is to simplify and clarify the path forward.

FORWARD AND ADAPTIVE BEATS STATIC AND SLOW

Finally, adaptability is key. Julie's focus on staying informed about industry trends and helping executives stay ahead of the curve shows how important it is for HR to be agile. In a rapidly changing business environment, forward-thinking HR strategies are vital.

Conclusion

My conversation with Julie reinforced what I've always believed—HR is a crucial driver of organizational success. Whether you're building trust with employees, supporting managers, or providing insights to senior leadership, your role is pivotal. By applying the five HR values and taking a strategic, people-first approach, you can ensure that HR remains a cornerstone of your company's growth and success.

When Talent Management Goes Awry: Engagement Is Not Happiness

I would be remiss if I didn't address a common misconception in the field of HR and talent management: the idea that employee engagement is synonymous with employee happiness. While both are important, they are not the same, and confusing the two can lead to significant challenges for organizations. Understanding this distinction is crucial for developing effective talent management strategies.

As senior HR leaders, our role is to ensure that our talent management practices drive both engagement and performance. It's essential to recognize that while happiness can contribute to a positive work environment, engagement is what truly drives productivity and organizational success. Let's explore why it's problematic to equate engagement with happiness and how we can address this issue.

Understanding Engagement vs. Happiness

WHAT IS ENGAGEMENT?

Employee engagement is about the emotional commitment an employee has to their organization and its goals. Engaged employees are motivated to contribute to the success of the company and are willing to put in extra effort to achieve that success. Engagement encompasses aspects like involvement in work, a sense of purpose, and a connection to the company's mission and values.

WHAT IS HAPPINESS?

Employee happiness, on the other hand, is about how satisfied employees are with their work environment, benefits, and day-to-day experiences. Happiness can be influenced by perks, work–life balance, and relationships with colleagues. While important, happiness alone does not necessarily translate to higher productivity or commitment to organizational goals.

Why the Confusion Is Problematic

SHORT-TERM VS. LONG-TERM FOCUS

Focusing solely on employee happiness can lead to short-term boosts in morale but may not result in long-term engagement. For example, offering free snacks or casual Fridays can make employees happy temporarily, but these perks do not necessarily foster a deep connection to the company's mission or encourage employees to go above and beyond in their roles.

POTENTIAL FOR COMPLACENCY

Prioritizing happiness without addressing engagement can lead to complacency. Employees might be content with their work environment but lack the drive to innovate or improve their performance. This complacency can hinder the organization's ability to remain competitive and achieve its strategic objectives. For instance, an employee who enjoys the work atmosphere but is not challenged by their tasks may not contribute to the company's growth or improvement.

MISALIGNED STRATEGIES

Confusing engagement with happiness can result in misaligned talent management strategies. Programs aimed solely at increasing happiness might overlook crucial elements that drive engagement, such as opportunities for professional development, meaningful work, and recognition of achievements. For example, focusing too much on recreational activities without providing career growth opportunities can lead to high turnover among ambitious employees seeking development.

Strategies to Foster True Engagement

MEANINGFUL WORK

To foster true engagement, we must focus on creating meaningful work experiences for employees. This involves ensuring that their roles are challenging, rewarding, and aligned with the organization's goals. For example, providing employees with opportunities to work on projects that have a significant impact on the company's success can enhance their sense of purpose and commitment.

PROFESSIONAL DEVELOPMENT

Investing in professional development is key to driving engagement. Offering training programs, mentorship, and career advancement opportunities helps employees grow and feel valued. For instance, implementing a leadership development program can prepare employees for future roles and demonstrate the organization's commitment to their long-term success.

RECOGNITION AND FEEDBACK

Regular recognition and constructive feedback are crucial for maintaining engagement. Recognizing employees' achievements and providing feedback on their performance reinforces their connection to the organization's goals and motivates them to continue contributing at a high level. For example, a formal recognition program that highlights employees' contributions can boost morale and encourage continued excellence.

EMPLOYEE INVOLVEMENT

Involving employees in decision-making processes can enhance their engagement by making them feel valued and heard. Soliciting their input on projects, policies, and changes within the organization demonstrates trust and respect. For example, creating employee committees or focus groups to provide feedback on company initiatives can increase their sense of ownership and commitment.

In summary, while employee happiness is important, it should not be confused with engagement. Engagement is about the emotional commitment employees have to the organization and its goals, and it drives productivity and long-term success. By focusing on meaningful work, professional development, recognition, and employee involvement, we can foster true engagement.

> I encourage you to evaluate your current talent management practices and ensure that they are designed to drive engagement, not just happiness. By doing so, you can create a motivated, committed workforce that contributes to the long-term success of your organization.

CASE STUDY EXERCISE

Adjusting Talent Management Strategies for Productivity

You are the HR Director at Community Care Network (CCN), a non profit organization dedicated to improving the wellbeing of local communities through various outreach programs. Your team is deeply passionate about the mission and is generally happy with their work environment. However, you've noticed that despite their enthusiasm and contentment, productivity levels are not meeting organizational goals. To address this issue, you need to adjust your talent management strategies to enhance productivity while maintaining high levels of employee engagement and satisfaction.

Please note: This case study is entirely fictitious. Any relationship to a real-world organization or person is entirely coincidental.

Task

Develop a comprehensive plan to adjust the talent management strategies at CCN. Your plan should focus on identifying the root causes of low productivity, implementing changes to improve performance, and ensuring that employees remain engaged and committed to the mission.

Supporting Questions

- What potential factors could be contributing to the low productivity levels at CCN despite high employee satisfaction?
- What steps can you take to ensure that employees have a clear understanding of their roles and performance expectations?
- What professional development opportunities can you offer to enhance employees' skills and competencies?
- How can you encourage a culture of continuous improvement where employees are motivated to enhance their performance?
- What recognition and reward mechanisms can you implement to reinforce positive behaviors and achievements?

Talent Management Checklist:
Daily, Weekly, Monthly, Quarterly, and Annual Activities

Daily Activities

ENGAGE WITH EMPLOYEES

Daily engagement with employees is crucial for building relationships and understanding their needs. Make it a habit to have informal conversations, whether in person or virtually, to gauge employee sentiment and gather feedback. This ongoing interaction helps build trust and keeps you informed about any emerging issues or concerns.

MONITOR PERFORMANCE

Regularly review performance metrics and attendance records to identify any immediate concerns. Keeping an eye on these indicators allows you to address potential issues promptly and ensures that employees remain productive and engaged.

Weekly Activities

TEAM MEETINGS

Hold weekly HR team meetings to discuss ongoing projects, share updates, and align on strategies. These meetings provide an opportunity to address any challenges, celebrate successes, and ensure everyone is on the same page.

CHECK-INS WITH MANAGERS

Schedule weekly check-ins with department managers to stay informed about their team's performance and any HR-related concerns. This regular communication helps identify potential issues early and supports managers in effectively leading their teams.

REVIEW PROGRESS

Take time each week to review the progress of ongoing HR initiatives. Assess whether they are on track to meet their goals and make any necessary adjustments. This ensures that your efforts remain aligned with the organization's strategic objectives.

Monthly Activities

EMPLOYEE FEEDBACK

Conduct monthly surveys or feedback sessions to gather insights from employees about their experiences and satisfaction levels. Analyzing this feedback helps identify areas for improvement and informs your talent management strategies.

PROFESSIONAL DEVELOPMENT

Plan and organize monthly training sessions or workshops to support employee development. Providing regular opportunities for learning and growth helps keep employees engaged and enhances their skills and competencies.

PERFORMANCE REVIEWS

Review and update performance management processes to ensure they are effective and aligned with organizational goals. Conducting regular performance reviews helps maintain a high level of performance and addresses any issues promptly.

Quarterly Activities

STRATEGIC ALIGNMENT

Assess the alignment of HR initiatives with the organization's quarterly goals. Ensure that your talent management strategies support these goals and adjust your plans as needed to maintain alignment.

STAKEHOLDER REPORTS

Prepare and present quarterly reports on HR initiatives and their impact to senior leadership and other stakeholders. These reports should include key metrics, success stories, and areas for improvement.

EMPLOYEE ENGAGEMENT ACTIVITIES

Organize quarterly employee engagement activities, such as team-building events or recognition ceremonies. These activities help foster a positive work environment and reinforce the organization's commitment to its employees.

Annual Activities

COMPREHENSIVE REVIEW

Conduct an annual review of all HR initiatives and their effectiveness. This comprehensive assessment helps identify what worked well and what needs improvement, informing your strategy for the coming year.

STRATEGIC PLANNING

Develop and set HR goals and strategies for the upcoming year. Align these goals with the organization's strategic objectives and allocate resources accordingly to support their achievement.

POLICY REVIEW

Review and update HR policies and procedures to ensure they are up-to-date and effective. This annual review helps maintain compliance with legal requirements and supports best practices in talent management.

EMPLOYEE SURVEY

Conduct a comprehensive employee engagement survey to gather in-depth feedback. Analyze the results and develop action plans to address any identified issues, ensuring that employee voices are heard and valued.

PROFESSIONAL DEVELOPMENT PLANNING

Identify and pursue opportunities for professional development in communication for HR staff. Encourage team members to complete relevant certifications and courses to enhance their skills and knowledge.

In summary, a structured Talent Management Checklist ensures that we consistently engage in activities that drive employee engagement, performance, and organizational success. By following these daily, weekly, monthly, quarterly, and annual activities, we can maintain a proactive and strategic approach to talent management.

I encourage you to integrate this checklist into your routine and customize it to fit your organization's needs. By doing so, you can enhance your talent management practices and contribute more effectively to your organization's long-term success.

Reflections on Talent: How Are You Shaping Your Workforce?

When thinking about how HR shapes the workforce, talent management is the foundation. Your talent management initiatives must directly support the strategic objectives of the company and help the organization deliver its brand promises to internal and external stakeholders alike. It's not enough to simply attract and retain employees; the people you bring in should help move the organization toward its goals. This requires a thoughtful approach, where recruitment, onboarding, development, and performance management are rooted into the company's broader vision. Owning your expertise means taking the lead in this alignment, using data and strategic insights to ensure that the way your organization hires, develops, and retains its workforce remains a key driver of organizational success.

Attracting the right talent begins with understanding what makes your organization unique. What draws people to your company, and how are you positioning yourself in the marketplace? The best strategies go beyond flashy perks and focus on showcasing the core of your culture and mission. Once employees are on board, the process of integration is key. Onboarding should be designed not just to train employees on their tasks but to immerse them in the culture. Igniting the spark in new employees through an engaging onboarding process ensures that they connect deeply with the company's purpose from day one.

Employee development is an ongoing commitment. It's not just about offering training programs but creating clear paths for career growth that align with both the company's needs and individual aspirations. Being part coach, part cheerleader, HR should foster an environment where employees feel supported in their development, with regular feedback and opportunities to grow. Your performance management system plays a vital role here—feedback must be constructive, consistent, and actionable, helping employees improve and contribute to the company's success.

Engagement is the fuel that powers productivity, and without it, even the most talented employees will fall short. HR should be proactive in measuring engagement and identifying areas where improvement is needed. Are employees connected to the company's mission? Do they feel valued? Bringing clarity from the clouds, HR can address engagement issues head-on by identifying root causes and implementing targeted strategies to improve morale and motivation.

Retention is just as critical as attraction, and retaining the right talent requires a deep understanding of what drives employees to stay or leave your organization. Use exit interviews and stay interviews to gather feedback and make informed changes. Succession planning is another area where forward and adaptive HR practices are essential. A robust succession plan ensures leadership continuity and allows the company to grow without the disruption of talent gaps.

Finally, innovation in talent management is key to keeping your strategies fresh and competitive. Are you exploring new ways to attract, retain, and engage employees? Whether it's through the use of data and analytics or by promoting diversity and inclusion, innovation ensures that HR remains a strategic partner in shaping the company's workforce. The best HR leaders are always looking for ways to improve, adapt, and drive the business forward.

> Regularly reflecting on these questions can help you identify strengths and areas for improvement in your talent management practices. Use these insights to drive more effective and impactful talent management strategies.

Conclusion

As we close this chapter, I hope you recognize the immense power you wield as an HR leader in managing talent strategically. Your role goes beyond policies and procedures—it's about shaping a workforce that is engaged, capable, and aligned with the organization's vision. By embracing data analytics, fostering continuous improvement, and developing comprehensive onboarding and retention strategies, you can directly impact the organization's success. Never underestimate the influence of HR: your work is pivotal in driving positive change, growth, and resilience across the business.

Reference

Price, J (2012) Study: U.S. Job Seekers Want Growth, Professional Development, Jumpstart HR, jumpstart-hr.com/study-u-s-job-seekers-want-growth-profes-sional-development/ (archived at https://perma.cc/PJ9S-WQ5A)

7

Recruitment and Onboarding

Introduction

In the realm of HR, recruitment and onboarding stand as foundational pillars that shape not just the employee experience but the overall success of an organization. The ability to attract, hire, and seamlessly integrate new talent is crucial in today's highly competitive market. This chapter delves into these pivotal HR functions, exploring how clear communication, effective branding, and a well-structured onboarding process can make a significant impact. The example of Malik, a fictional job seeker whose recruitment journey transformed his career, underscores the importance of these practices.

As HR professionals, our role is not just about filling positions but about strategically aligning recruitment and onboarding efforts with broader organizational goals. When done right, this process fosters engagement, loyalty, and productivity from day one.

We'll explore key strategies like building a strong employer brand, utilizing data-driven recruitment practices, and fostering an inclusive, engaging candidate experience. Additionally, we'll emphasize the importance of post-hire support, demonstrating how thoughtful onboarding can set the stage for long-term success. The practices and tools covered here aren't just theoretical—they offer a roadmap for how HR can lead talent acquisition efforts that are proactive, strategic, and aligned with the ever-evolving needs of the business.

Let's begin the chapter with an example of how personal attention, clear communication, and thoughtful onboarding practices create strong first impressions. The fictional letter from Malik, a job seeker turned new hire, illustrates how a seamless candidate journey can build trust, confidence, and long-term success. Through tailored recruitment and ongoing support, HR professionals play a pivotal role in shaping not only careers but also the culture and future success of our organizations.

First Impressions: A Tale of Onboarding Done Right

Dear Pamela,

I hope this letter finds you well. I wanted to take a moment to express my profound gratitude for the exceptional support and guidance you provided during my recent job search. After two years of seeking employment, I am thrilled to have landed my dream job, and I truly believe that your efforts made all the difference.

As you know, I had sold my business just prior to the Covid-19 pandemic, and while I was fortunate to have built up a significant amount of savings, those funds were dwindling quickly due to the need to cover medical expenses for my son. The pressure to find a stable position to ensure my family's financial security was immense. Your support throughout this journey has been invaluable.

As a former CEO, I strongly believe in the importance of feedback. Here are a few aspects of the candidate experience that stood out to me and which I believe were instrumental in securing this opportunity.

Personalized and Transparent Communication

From our first interaction, you took the time to understand my unique background and aspirations. Your personalized approach made me feel valued and confident that I was more than just another resume. The transparent communication about the hiring process and what to expect at each stage was reassuring and helped me manage my expectations effectively.

Comprehensive Preparation for Interviews

The detailed insights you provided about the company culture, team dynamics, and the specific role were incredibly helpful. The mock interview sessions and the feedback you offered boosted my confidence and allowed me to present my best self. Knowing what the interviewers were looking for and being well-prepared for their questions made a significant difference.

Thoughtful Onboarding Experience

Once I received the job offer, the onboarding process was seamless. The clear and structured plan you provided helped me transition smoothly into my new role. The welcome package, including resources about the company's values, expectations, and initial training materials, was a thoughtful touch that made me feel part of the team from day one.

Continuous Support and Follow-Up

Your ongoing support didn't end with the job offer. The regular check-ins during my initial weeks on the job made me feel supported and assured that I had someone to turn to if any issues arose. Your dedication to ensuring my successful integration into the company speaks volumes about your commitment to candidates' long-term success.

After a prolonged period of uncertainty and financial strain, finding this role has brought much-needed stability to my family. Your professionalism, empathy, and expertise have not only helped me secure employment but have also restored my confidence and optimism about the future.

Thank you once again for your outstanding support. I am genuinely excited about this new chapter in my life and am deeply grateful for the role you played in making it possible.

With heartfelt appreciation,

Malik

Attracting the Best: Strategies for Effective Recruitment

Attracting the best talent is not just about filling positions, it's about finding individuals who will drive your company's mission forward and help achieve your strategic goals. Effective recruitment strategies are essential for building a high-performing, innovative, and committed workforce.

When you are a senior HR or Talent Acquisition leader, you play a pivotal role in shaping the future of your organization through your recruitment practices. Our ability to attract top talent directly affects our organization's capacity to grow, innovate, and compete. Let's delve into the strategies that can help us attract the best candidates and ensure a successful recruitment process.

Understanding the Importance of Recruitment

Effective recruitment begins with understanding and aligning with the organization's strategic objectives. This alignment ensures that we are not just hiring to fill immediate needs but also building a workforce that supports long-term goals. For example, if our goal is to expand into new markets, we need to recruit individuals with the skills and experience to drive that expansion.

Building a Strong Employer Brand

A strong employer brand is essential for attracting top talent. It represents your organization's culture, values, and mission. Candidates today are not just looking for a job; they are looking for a place where they can align their personal values with the company's mission. Developing and promoting a compelling employer brand can help you stand out in a competitive job market. And when you build an effective employer brand, candidates will come. According to LinkedIn Talent Solutions (LinkedIn Talent Solutions, n.d.), companies see a 28 percent reduction in turnover, a 50 percent cost-per-hire reduction, and 1–2x faster time to hire.

Strategies to Enhance Employer Branding

SHOWCASING COMPANY CULTURE

Use social media, company websites, and other platforms to showcase your company culture. Highlight employee testimonials, behind-the-scenes glimpses of the workplace, and stories that reflect your organizational values.

ENGAGING CONTENT

Create engaging content that resonates with potential candidates. This can include blog posts, videos, and case studies that highlight the company's achievements, values, and opportunities for growth.

EMPLOYEE ADVOCACY

Encourage employees to share their positive experiences on social media and review sites. Employee advocacy is a powerful tool for building a credible employer brand.

Implementing Effective Recruitment Strategies

LEVERAGING TECHNOLOGY

Technology plays a crucial role in modern recruitment. Applicant Tracking Systems (ATS), AI-driven recruitment tools, and social media platforms can streamline the recruitment process, making it more efficient and effective. For example, using AI to screen resumes can save time and ensure that only the most qualified candidates move forward.

UTILIZING DATA AND ANALYTICS

Data-driven recruitment allows us to make informed decisions. By analyzing data from previous hiring cycles, we can identify what works and what doesn't. Metrics such as time-to-fill, cost-per-hire, and quality-of-hire provide valuable insights into the effectiveness of our recruitment strategies.

BUILDING TALENT PIPELINES

Proactively building talent pipelines ensures that we have a pool of qualified candidates ready when positions become available. This involves engaging with potential candidates long before a job opening arises. Networking, attending industry events, and maintaining relationships with past applicants can help build a strong talent pipeline.

EMPLOYEE REFERRAL PROGRAMS

Employee referrals are one of the most effective ways to find high-quality candidates. Employees who refer others typically bring in candidates who fit well with the company culture and have the necessary skills. Implementing a structured referral program with incentives can boost participation and yield excellent results.

INCLUSIVE RECRUITMENT PRACTICES

Diversity and inclusion should be at the forefront of our recruitment strategies. Creating an inclusive recruitment process ensures that we attract a diverse range of candidates, bringing varied perspectives and ideas into the organization. This can be achieved by using diverse job boards, writing inclusive job descriptions, and ensuring unbiased screening processes.

Ensuring a Positive Candidate Experience

CLEAR COMMUNICATION

Effective communication throughout the recruitment process is crucial. Keeping candidates informed about their application status, providing feedback, and outlining the next steps can significantly enhance their experience.

STREAMLINED PROCESSES

Simplifying and streamlining the application process reduces barriers for candidates. A lengthy or complicated application process can deter top talent from applying. Ensure that your application process is user-friendly and efficient.

PERSONAL TOUCH

Adding a personal touch, such as personalized emails or follow-up calls, shows candidates that they are valued. This can leave a lasting positive impression, even if they are not ultimately selected for the position.

In summary, attracting the best talent requires a strategic approach that aligns with organizational goals, builds a strong employer brand, leverages technology and data, fosters inclusive practices, and ensures a positive candidate experience. By implementing these strategies, we can effectively attract and retain top talent, driving our organization's success.

> I encourage you to review your current recruitment practices and identify areas for improvement. By adopting these strategies, you can enhance your recruitment processes and build a workforce that is committed, innovative, and aligned with your organizational goals.

Mentor's Corner: The Best Hire You'll Make Is the One You Don't Have To

In the fast-evolving landscape of HR and talent acquisition, one thing remains constant: the need to hire effectively. The challenge is not only in finding the right talent but also in retaining them long enough so you don't need to keep filling the same roles over and over again. Recently, I had the privilege of talking with Tim Sackett, a leader in talent acquisition and President of HRU Technical Resources, about how the world of recruitment has changed. The themes of speed, competition for talent, candidate-driven markets, and treating candidates like people—not numbers—are more important now than ever before. Are you up for the challenge?

As Tim and I spoke, one of the first things we discussed was how quickly the recruitment cycle moves today compared with when we both entered the field. In the past, you measured recruitment in weeks or months. Today, it's often a matter of days or even hours. The pace at which companies need to attract and hire talent has dramatically accelerated, and while technology has been a key enabler, it's also created a more complex system. The need for speed often clashes with the reality that good decision-making takes time, particularly when it comes to ensuring quality hires. This raises an important point: speed is critical, but it must be balanced with careful strategy to avoid poor hires.

Tim brings up another major change: how competition for talent has evolved. Years ago, companies had the luxury of thinking talent pools were theirs to tap into exclusively. You posted a job, people applied, and you had time to sift through resumes. Today, candidates are often applying to multiple roles simultaneously, and employers are in a fierce race to offer the best opportunities. The mindset that a candidate is only interested in your organization is no longer valid. Employers must now compete for the attention of top talent, and that means refining recruitment strategies to stand out in a crowded market.

This is where the importance of creating a strong, respectful candidate experience comes in. A key takeaway from my conversation with Tim is that while we should aim to create a positive experience for candidates, there's no need to overdo it with extravagant perks. Simple professionalism, clear communication, and treating candidates the way we'd want to be treated is often enough. As Tim says, the "golden rule" should apply here—treat others as you'd want to be treated. So often, companies fail at this. They drag candidates through endless interviews, ghost them at critical stages, or fail to communicate next steps.

The best companies, the ones that are succeeding in talent acquisition, are those that value the candidate's time and give them a sense of transparency in the process. In my opinion, if this is something your organization struggles with then it is the biggest issue you can improve to wildly transform your recruitment outcomes.

When we touched on the topic of multigenerational workplaces, the conversation turned to how each generation's expectations differ, not necessarily because of age but because of their life stages. Millennials who are balancing families and mortgages have different needs than Gen Z employees who are just beginning their careers. What struck me most was how we, as HR professionals, often underestimate the capacity of older employees to contribute significantly. The assumption is that younger employees will always produce more, but older employees often have the experience, stability, and time to dedicate to their work that can make them just as—if not more—valuable. You would be wise not to dismiss the valuable experience of older members of your workforce.

The conversation naturally led to one of the biggest questions in HR today: remote versus in-office work. The debate is often framed as generational, with younger workers preferring remote work, while older generations supposedly value being in the office. But Tim has an interesting take—it's not really about where you work, it's about where you work best. The key is to help employees find the environment where they are most productive and successful, and it will vary from person to person. HR's role in this is to help employees discover where they thrive, and this may require a more nuanced approach than simply offering one blanket policy. Additionally, I believe this requires you to empower managers to have the final say on where their team works—a call back to the decentralization of HR that Lars brought to our attention earlier in the book.

One of the final, and most insightful, points we discussed was the often-overlooked role recruiters play in the long-term employee experience. While many HR leaders think of recruiters as handling the "front end" of the employee life cycle, Tim argues that recruiters should maintain relationships with their hires well after they've started. It's about continuous re-recruitment. What if recruiters continued to check in on employees, helping them navigate their careers within the company? Imagine if every employee had someone in their corner, much like an agent, guiding them through internal opportunities and career growth. This would reduce turnover and make employees feel valued long after their initial hire date.

Applying the Five HR Values

Our discussion aligns beautifully with the five HR values I emphasize in this book time and time again.

OWN YOUR EXPERTISE

Whether it's navigating the speed of hiring or managing relationships with candidates, owning your expertise means taking charge of the recruitment process from start to finish. Tim talked about the importance of being transparent with senior leadership when hiring challenges arise. Instead of hiding behind delays, own the narrative and use your expertise to explain what's happening. In this way, HR doesn't just manage talent but drives the conversation on how to improve it.

BE PART COACH, PART CHEERLEADER

Tim's idea of recruiters maintaining relationships with hires long after they've been onboarded is a perfect example of this value. Imagine if HR took on the role of coach for employees, helping them navigate their career path within the company. Regular check-ins, career development advice, and guidance would ensure employees feel supported at every stage of their journey. This ongoing relationship fosters loyalty and boosts retention.

IGNITE THE SPARK

A positive candidate experience is a recruiter's chance to ignite the spark in prospective employees. By being respectful, timely, and transparent during the hiring process, HR professionals can instill a sense of excitement in candidates. As Tim points out, the best companies aren't the ones sending fruit baskets—they're the ones treating candidates like people. When you ignite that initial spark, it can carry over into the employee's long-term engagement with the organization because it sets a very powerful tone.

BRING CLARITY FROM THE CLOUDS

When discussing remote work versus in-office work, Tim shared that the key is to help employees understand where they work best. HR's job here is to bring clarity to what can be a murky situation. Instead of framing it as a binary decision—remote versus in-office—HR can help employees see where they thrive. This value is also essential when managing expectations in recruitment. Be clear about the process, communicate the steps, and make sure everyone knows what to expect.

FORWARD AND ADAPTIVE BEATS STATIC AND SLOW

The speed at which recruitment happens today exemplifies this value. We can't afford to be slow or stuck in outdated processes. Tim emphasized that the companies that adapt to this fast-paced environment are the ones that succeed. This doesn't mean sacrificing quality for speed; it means being adaptive and using technology and processes that allow for both. When recruitment is agile, the whole organization benefits.

Conclusion

My conversation with Tim Sackett reaffirmed what we've always known as HR leaders—HR is the engine behind every great hire and every great team. By embracing the values of expertise, coaching, clarity, and adaptability, HR professionals can not only attract top talent but also keep them engaged and growing within the organization. The best hire is indeed the one you don't have to make, and the key to getting there lies in treating recruitment as the start of a long, ongoing relationship. By focusing on how we treat candidates, how we support employees, and how we communicate with leadership, we ensure HR remains a pivotal force in organizational success.

Recruitment Challenges: Handling Difficult Scenarios

Recruitment is a critical function of HR, but it's not without its challenges. I want to address some of the most difficult scenarios I've faced in recruitment and discuss strategies for overcoming them. Effective recruitment is not just about attracting talent, it's about navigating obstacles and ensuring we find the right fit for our organization.

In order to find the right fit for our organization, it's crucial that we are equipped to handle these challenging scenarios with strategic approaches and practical solutions. By addressing these challenges head-on, we can improve our recruitment processes, enhance candidate experience, and ultimately build a stronger workforce. Let's explore five common recruitment challenges and how to overcome them.

Scenario 1: Attracting Talent in a Competitive Market

CHALLENGE

In highly competitive markets, attracting top talent can be particularly challenging. Candidates often have multiple offers and can afford to be selective.

SOLUTION

To stand out in a competitive market, you need to strengthen your employer brand. Highlight what makes your organization unique— whether it's your company culture, growth opportunities, or commitment to innovation. Additionally, offering competitive salaries and benefits is crucial. Engage with potential candidates through social media, industry events, and professional networks to build relationships before you need to hire. Showcasing employee testimonials and success stories can also help attract top talent.

Scenario 2: High Volume of Unqualified Applicants

CHALLENGE

Receiving a high volume of applicants, many of whom are unqualified, can overwhelm the recruitment team and slow down the hiring process, especially in a recruiting environment where candidates expect timely, personalized responses to their application.

SOLUTION

Implementing an Applicant Tracking System can streamline the process by filtering out unqualified candidates. Clearly defined job descriptions with specific qualifications and requirements can also help attract the right candidates. Use pre-screening questionnaires to assess basic qualifications before moving candidates to the next stage. Additionally, leveraging AI-driven tools can help identify the most promising candidates based on their resumes and application data.

Scenario 3: Lengthy Hiring Process

CHALLENGE

A prolonged hiring process can result in losing top candidates to faster-moving competitors and can create a negative candidate experience. In a competitive market, you have to assume that the best candidates are interviewing for multiple positions at any given time. When you find the right candidate, time is truly of the essence.

SOLUTION

Streamline your hiring process by identifying and eliminating unnecessary steps. Set clear timelines for each stage of the recruitment process and communicate them to candidates. Use technology to speed up processes, such as scheduling interviews and sharing feedback. Regularly review and adjust your process to ensure it remains efficient. Keeping candidates informed about their status and providing timely feedback can also improve their experience and keep them engaged.

Scenario 4: Managing Hiring Bias

CHALLENGE

Unconscious bias in recruitment can lead to a lack of diversity and inclusion, and may result in hiring the wrong candidates for the wrong reasons. It can also result in a stalled recruiting process if multiple biases rule out several qualified applicants for a role.

SOLUTION

Implement structured interview processes with standardized questions to ensure fairness. Use diverse hiring panels to bring multiple perspectives to the evaluation process. Provide training on unconscious bias for all individuals involved in the hiring process. Utilize blind hiring techniques, such as removing personal information from resumes during the initial screening, to focus on skills and qualifications. Regularly review your hiring data to identify and address any biases.

Scenario 5: Candidate Drop-Off During the Recruitment Process

CHALLENGE

Candidates dropping out of the recruitment process midway can disrupt hiring plans and extend the time to fill positions.

SOLUTION

Ensure a positive candidate experience by maintaining clear and consistent communication throughout the process. Simplify the application process to make it user-friendly and avoid unnecessary steps. Provide candidates with realistic job previews to set accurate expectations. Engage candidates by offering insights into the company culture, team dynamics, and growth opportunities. Follow up promptly after each stage to keep candidates informed and engaged. Consider pay transparency in your job descriptions so that applicants are not surprised by what compensation you can offer in the role.

In summary, recruitment challenges are inevitable, but with the right strategies, we can overcome them effectively. Strengthening our employer brand, utilizing technology, streamlining processes, addressing bias, and maintaining clear communication are key to handling these difficult scenarios.

I encourage you to assess your current recruitment practices and implement these strategies to tackle the challenges you face. By doing so, you can enhance your recruitment processes, improve candidate experiences, and build a diverse and talented workforce.

CASE STUDY EXERCISE

Removing Stumbling Blocks for a New Manager Recruiting for the First Time

You are the HR Director at EcoTech Solutions, a rapidly growing company specializing in sustainable technology. Recently, a new manager, Jane, has joined the company and is tasked with building her team. This is Jane's first experience with recruiting, and she is encountering several stumbling blocks, including crafting job descriptions, screening candidates, conducting interviews, and making hiring decisions. Your role is to provide guidance and support to help Jane navigate these challenges and successfully recruit top talent for her team.

Please note: This case study is entirely fictitious. Any relationship to a real-world organization or person is entirely coincidental.

Task

Develop a comprehensive plan to support Jane in her recruitment efforts. Your plan should address the key stumbling blocks she is facing and provide actionable strategies and resources to overcome them.

Supporting Questions

- What are the essential components of an effective job description?
- What criteria should Jane use to screen resumes and applications effectively?
- How can Jane ensure that her interview questions are fair, unbiased, and aligned with the job requirements?
- What factors should Jane consider when making a hiring decision?
- What resources and training can you provide to help Jane develop her recruiting skills?

Recruitment and Onboarding Checklist: Your Go-To Guide

To ensure the success of your recruitment and onboarding processes, it is essential to maintain a structured and consistent approach. This checklist outlines daily, weekly, monthly, quarterly, and annual activities to help you manage recruitment and onboarding effectively.

Daily Activities

MONITOR JOB POSTINGS

- Review and update job postings on various platforms to ensure accuracy and attractiveness.
- Respond promptly to inquiries from potential candidates.

SCREEN APPLICATIONS

- Conduct an initial review of incoming resumes and applications to identify promising candidates.
- Schedule pre-screening calls or interviews with qualified candidates.

ENGAGE WITH CANDIDATES

- Maintain regular communication with candidates in the pipeline to keep them informed and engaged.
- Provide timely responses to candidate questions and concerns.

TRACK RECRUITMENT METRICS

- Monitor daily recruitment metrics, such as the number of applications received and candidate progress through the hiring pipeline.

Weekly Activities

TEAM MEETINGS

- Hold weekly recruitment team meetings to discuss ongoing job openings, candidate status, and any challenges faced.
- Review and prioritize recruitment needs and strategies.

CANDIDATE INTERVIEWS

- Schedule and conduct interviews with candidates, ensuring a diverse interview panel.
- Collect and review feedback from interviewers to make informed decisions.

UPDATE HIRING MANAGERS

- Provide weekly updates to hiring managers on the status of their open positions and candidate progress.
- Seek feedback from hiring managers to refine the recruitment process.

REVIEW JOB DESCRIPTIONS

- Ensure job descriptions are up-to-date and accurately reflect the requirements and responsibilities of the positions.

Monthly Activities

PERFORMANCE REVIEW

- Review the performance of recruitment efforts, including time-to-fill, cost-per-hire, and quality-of-hire metrics.
- Identify areas for improvement and adjust strategies accordingly.

TALENT PIPELINE DEVELOPMENT

- Proactively build and maintain a talent pipeline by networking with potential candidates and attending industry events.
- Engage with passive candidates to keep them interested in future opportunities.

TRAINING AND DEVELOPMENT

- Provide training sessions for recruiters and hiring managers on best practices, interview techniques, and using recruitment tools.
- Stay updated on industry trends and new recruitment technologies.

EMPLOYEE REFERRAL PROGRAM

- Review and promote the employee referral program to encourage employees to refer qualified candidates.
- Track the success of referrals and provide incentives for successful hires.

Quarterly Activities

STRATEGIC ALIGNMENT

- Review the alignment of recruitment strategies with organizational goals and adjust plans as needed.
- Meet with senior leadership to discuss upcoming hiring needs and priorities.

STAKEHOLDER REPORTS

- Prepare and present quarterly reports on recruitment efforts, including key metrics and success stories.
- Share insights and recommendations with senior leadership and other stakeholders.

ONBOARDING REVIEW

- Evaluate the effectiveness of the onboarding process and gather feedback from recent hires.
- Implement improvements to ensure a smooth and engaging onboarding experience.

DIVERSITY AND INCLUSION INITIATIVES

- Review recruitment practices to ensure they promote diversity and inclusion.
- Implement initiatives to attract and hire a diverse workforce.

Annual Activities

COMPREHENSIVE REVIEW

- Conduct an annual review of recruitment and onboarding strategies and their effectiveness.
- Identify strengths, weaknesses, and areas for improvement.

STRATEGIC PLANNING

- Develop recruitment goals and strategies for the upcoming year, aligned with organizational objectives.
- Allocate resources and budget for recruitment activities.

POLICY AND PROCESS REVIEW

- Review and update recruitment policies and procedures to ensure they are current and effective.
- Ensure compliance with legal and regulatory requirements.

EMPLOYEE ENGAGEMENT SURVEY

- Conduct an annual employee engagement survey to gather feedback on the recruitment and onboarding process.

- Use the results to inform improvements and enhance the candidate experience.

PROFESSIONAL DEVELOPMENT

- Encourage recruiters and hiring managers to pursue professional development opportunities, such as certifications and training programs.
- Stay informed about industry best practices and emerging trends.

This checklist provides a structured approach to managing recruitment and onboarding processes effectively. By breaking down activities into daily, weekly, monthly, quarterly, and annual tasks, you can maintain consistency and drive continuous improvement.

> I encourage you to integrate this checklist into your routine and customize it to fit your organization's needs. By doing so, you can enhance your recruitment and onboarding practices and build a strong, engaged workforce.

Thinking Ahead: How Can You Improve Recruiting and Onboarding Processes?

In today's fast-paced business world, aligning recruitment strategies with organizational goals is paramount. As HR leaders, it's our responsibility to ensure that the people we bring into our organization are not just skilled in their positions but instrumental in driving the company's success. By regularly reviewing how well our hiring processes allow the organization to meet its objectives, we can refine our strategies to better meet current and future needs.

Employer branding plays a key role in this alignment. A strong employer brand can be the differentiator in attracting top-tier talent, especially in competitive industries. The brand isn't just about advertising perks or highlighting a positive work environment; it's about demonstrating a clear alignment with the company's mission and values. If we want to be viewed as an employer of choice, we need to communicate that consistently and authentically to potential candidates. Moreover, it must be an accurate reflection of the promises made and delivered to members of our teams.

Another critical aspect of recruitment is the candidate experience. How we communicate with candidates throughout the hiring process shapes their perception of our organization, whether they join the team or not. Timely, clear communication helps to build trust and can leave a positive impression even if a candidate isn't selected. Collecting feedback from candidates who have gone through our process, whether successful or not, is vital for continuous improvement. If we find areas of dissatisfaction, we should address them promptly to improve the overall experience.

Leveraging technology is another area ripe for optimization. Data and analytics are powerful tools that can help streamline recruitment processes and offer insights into where we might improve. By investing in the right technology, we can reduce inefficiencies, speed up time-to-hire, and ensure we're making data-driven decisions that lead to better hires.

Diversity and inclusion must remain at the forefront of our recruitment efforts. It's easy to fall into comfortable patterns when hiring, but creating a truly diverse workforce requires intention. Reviewing our recruitment practices regularly for biases and ensuring that our job postings, interviews, and hiring processes are inclusive will help attract a wider pool of talent.

Efficiency in recruitment matters too. Time-to-fill is often a key metric for success in recruitment, but it shouldn't come at the expense of candidate quality. Identifying bottlenecks in the hiring process and addressing them can lead to faster, more efficient hiring while maintaining high standards.

Onboarding, often overlooked, is just as crucial as the recruitment process itself. Effective onboarding ensures that new hires are integrated smoothly and feel like part of the team from day one. Gathering feedback from new employees about their onboarding experience helps us continuously refine our approach, ensuring we set new hires up for long-term success.

An employee referral program is a valuable tool in recruiting quality candidates. According to FitSmallBusiness.com, people who are referred by current employees tend to be better cultural fits and have higher retention rates (Soper, 2023). Encouraging employees to participate in the referral program and recognizing their contributions when referrals lead to successful hires can significantly improve the program's effectiveness.

Training is another cornerstone of successful recruitment. Recruiters and hiring managers should be well-versed in best practices and should regularly participate in training to mitigate unconscious bias. Ongoing development ensures that our recruitment teams stay sharp and aligned with the company's goals.

Finally, continuous improvement is key. Regularly gathering feedback, whether from candidates, new hires, or hiring managers, helps us refine our processes. Fostering a culture of improvement within the HR team encourages innovation and ensures we are always looking for ways to enhance our recruitment and onboarding strategies.

By applying the five HR values—Own Your Expertise; Be Part Coach, Part Cheerleader; Ignite the Spark; Bring Clarity From the Clouds; and Forward and Adaptive Beats Static and Slow—we can create a recruitment and onboarding process that truly drives organizational success.

> Regularly reflecting on these questions can help you identify strengths and areas for improvement in your recruitment and onboarding practices. Use these insights to drive more effective and impactful strategies.

Conclusion

As we conclude this chapter, it's clear that recruitment and onboarding are far more than transactional processes. They are strategic endeavors that, when done well, can shape the future of the organization. By aligning recruitment practices with business objectives, fostering a strong employer brand, and emphasizing clear, thoughtful communication, HR professionals can elevate both the candidate experience and long-term employee engagement. Onboarding should not end with an orientation session; it must be an ongoing journey of support, feedback, and development. Ensuring new hires feel welcomed, valued, and set up for success from day one is a cornerstone of effective HR practices.

Ultimately, the HR leader's role in this process is both tactical and transformative. By owning our expertise, being proactive in coaching and supporting new hires, and continuously improving our processes, we drive not just talent acquisition but organizational growth. The strategies outlined in this chapter, when applied consistently and thoughtfully, can ensure that we are not only hiring for immediate needs but building a robust workforce equipped to meet the challenges of the future.

References

LinkedIn Talent Solutions (n.d.) The Ultimate List of Employer Brand Statistics: For Hiring Managers, HR Professionals, and Recruiters, LinkedIn, business. linkedin.com/content/dam/business/talent-solutions/global/en_us/c/pdfs/ ultimate-list-of-employer-brand-stats.pdf (archived at https://perma.cc/E4FE-H4UN)

Soper, J (2023) How to Create an Employee Referral Program [+ Template], Fit Small Business, fitsmallbusiness.com/employee-referrals/ (archived at https://perma.cc/EE6D-GGLY)

8

Employee Engagement
and Retention

Introduction

Employee engagement and retention aren't just checkboxes on an HR agenda—they are necessary for an organization's success. In today's fast-paced, competitive environment, companies that focus on understanding and retaining their talent gain a powerful advantage. The connection between engagement and retention is clear: engaged employees are more productive, more innovative, and more likely to stay long-term. This chapter takes you through the pivotal strategies that influence engagement, from fostering a positive work environment to offering clear career development paths. Through thoughtful leadership, transparent communication, and the use of meaningful employee feedback, HR professionals can create workplaces where employees thrive and stay loyal. We'll explore practical approaches to building a culture of engagement, reviewing retention practices, and ensuring alignment with overall business goals. Engaging and retaining top talent is not just about avoiding turnover—it's about building an environment where employees feel valued, connected, and inspired to contribute to the organization's mission every day.

In our opening fictional story, we follow Mark Thompson, an employee at Pinnacle Industries. Mark proudly reflects on how HR's dedication to engagement and inclusivity has shaped his experience as a physically-disabled worker. Through personalized support and initiatives that prioritize accessibility and growth, Mark's journey showcases the transformative power of thoughtful HR leadership.

Engagement Stories: The Heart of Organizational Success

Mark Thompson had been working at Pinnacle Industries for nearly a decade. As someone who uses a wheelchair, he always felt a bit nervous starting new jobs, unsure of how accessible the work environment would be. But at Pinnacle, things were different. From the moment he joined, the HR team made sure every part of his onboarding and continued engagement was seamless. The company had an unwavering commitment to accessibility and inclusivity, and Mark noticed it wasn't just lip service.

Mark remembered his first day. HR had already ensured his workspace was accessible, and they scheduled a meeting with the IT team to discuss adaptive technology that could enhance his productivity. HR continuously checked in—not to meet quotas or legal requirements, but because they genuinely cared about his experience.

One thing that really stood out to Mark was the company's approach to employee engagement. HR, in collaboration with leadership, implemented programs designed to support all employees—whether disabled or not—by focusing on personal growth and development. They hosted frequent feedback sessions, created opportunities for mentorship, and provided professional development that catered to individual strengths and needs.

Mark often participated in the engagement surveys HR sent out. The questions were meaningful and the responses were always taken seriously. He noticed that suggestions he and his colleagues made were regularly implemented. HR wasn't just focused on productivity—they were focused on making the workplace a true community. When Mark's department launched a new initiative to foster leadership opportunities for disabled employees, HR's support was immediate and wholehearted. They worked tirelessly to break down any barriers and ensure that every employee had a voice.

Ten years later, Mark reflected on his time at Pinnacle Industries with pride. HR's dedication to improving engagement didn't just help him succeed, it made him feel valued as an individual. It was why he was still there and thriving. HR had shaped a culture that proved every employee, regardless of their challenges, could achieve great things when given the right support.

The Engagement Equation: What Drives Employee Loyalty

Employee engagement and loyalty is the goal that every employer strives for. Employee engagement is not just a buzzword, it is a vital component of a thriving, productive workplace. Understanding what drives employee loyalty allows us to create an environment where employees are motivated, committed, and aligned with the organization's goals.

It is our responsibility to foster a culture of engagement that drives loyalty and performance. Employee loyalty leads to lower turnover rates, higher productivity, and a more cohesive work environment. Let's explore the key factors that drive employee loyalty and how we can harness them to build a more engaged workforce.

Understanding Employee Engagement

Employee engagement refers to the emotional commitment employees have to their organization and its goals. I often say that engaged employees are not just satisfied with their jobs, they are motivated to go above and beyond to contribute to the organization's success. This level of engagement is crucial because it directly impacts productivity, customer satisfaction, and overall business performance.

Key Factors Driving Employee Loyalty

MEANINGFUL WORK

The Role of Purpose   One of the most significant drivers of employee engagement and loyalty is the sense of purpose that comes from meaningful work. When employees understand how their roles contribute to the larger mission of the organization, they are more likely to feel connected and committed. For example, at a non profit organization, employees who see the direct impact of their work on the community are often highly engaged and loyal.

Strategies to Implement   To foster a sense of purpose, communicate the organization's mission and values clearly and frequently. Ensure that employees understand how their work aligns with the broader goals of the company. Providing opportunities for employees to see the impact of their contributions, such as through customer feedback or success stories, can also enhance their sense of purpose.

RECOGNITION AND APPRECIATION

The Power of Recognition   Recognizing and appreciating employees' efforts is a powerful motivator. Employees who feel valued are more likely to stay loyal to the organization. Recognition can take many forms, from formal awards and bonuses to simple thank-you notes and public acknowledgment.

Strategies to Implement   Create a culture of recognition by implementing regular recognition programs. Encourage managers and peers to acknowledge each other's achievements. Use both formal and informal methods to show appreciation, and ensure that recognition is specific, timely, and aligned with organizational values.

OPPORTUNITIES FOR GROWTH AND DEVELOPMENT

Importance of Development   Employees who see a clear path for career advancement are more likely to remain loyal. Providing opportunities for professional growth and development shows employees that the organization is invested in their future.

Strategies to Implement   Offer a variety of development opportunities, such as training programs, workshops, and mentoring. Create individual development plans (IDPs) that align employees' career goals with the organization's needs. Encourage continuous learning and provide resources for skill development.

POSITIVE WORK ENVIRONMENT

Creating a Supportive Culture   A positive work environment where employees feel supported, respected, and included is essential for driving engagement and loyalty. A culture of trust and collaboration fosters strong relationships and a sense of belonging.

Strategies to Implement   Promote a positive work environment by encouraging open communication and teamwork. Implement policies that support work–life balance, such as flexible working arrangements. Foster an inclusive culture where diversity is valued and everyone feels respected.

EFFECTIVE LEADERSHIP

The Impact of Leadership   Effective leadership is a critical factor in driving employee engagement and loyalty. Leaders who are supportive, transparent, and inspiring can significantly influence employees' commitment to the organization.

Strategies to Implement   Develop leadership skills at all levels of the organization. Provide training and support for managers to enhance their leadership capabilities. Encourage leaders to communicate openly, set clear expectations, and provide regular feedback.

In summary, the key drivers of employee loyalty include meaningful work, recognition and appreciation, opportunities for growth and development, a positive work environment, and effective leadership. By focusing on these factors, we can create a culture of engagement that drives loyalty and performance.

I encourage you to assess your current employee engagement strategies and identify areas for improvement. By implementing these strategies, you can foster a more engaged and loyal workforce, leading to greater organizational success.

Mentor's Corner: "We're Losing Money and We're Losing Talent"

In my conversation with Tony Butler-Sims, Senior VP and Chief People Officer at CNFA, we explored some critical perspectives on employee engagement and retention. The key takeaway? If we're not actively listening to our employees, we're doing them—and our organization—a disservice. Tony believes that it is crucial to not only gather feedback but also act on it transparently. If you're not ready to address employee concerns head-on, you shouldn't be asking them in the first place. Employee engagement is no longer just about listening; it's about creating trust, building relationships, and responding to the workforce in meaningful ways.

Tony's background in both the military and corporate sectors provided an insightful contrast. In the military, feedback flowed from the top down. But today's workforce, especially with younger generations, expects more openness, dialogue, and mutual acceptance of ideas. Employees now have strong voices, and their expectations go beyond just financial rewards—workplace flexibility, inclusivity, and trust are essential factors. One thing Tony emphasizes is the growing divide between leadership and employees if communication is neglected.

Engagement isn't just a "nice-to-have," it directly impacts retention, talent acquisition, and even profitability. Companies that don't actively engage their staff risk losing more than just good people—they lose money, time, and credibility. Tony urges us to know that recruiting is costly, but what's even more expensive is replacing talent due to disengagement. By instituting employee engagement strategies—whether through exit interviews, open-door policies, or retention bonuses—leaders can create an environment that fosters loyalty and trust.

At CNFA, Tony has overseen various employee retention strategies, including developing an innovative employee retention plan. His team created an initiative that rewards employees who stay for ten or more years, providing a cash incentive based on salary. This wasn't limited to executives; it was an inclusive effort to show that long-term commitment to the organization is valued at all levels. Tony made it clear that engagement goes beyond surveys and perks— it's about aligning values, ensuring communication, and, most importantly, building a culture of trust and openness.

Applying the Five HR Values

The five HR values apply here as well. Let's break them down.

OWN YOUR EXPERTISE

As Tony mentioned, HR leaders must be the bridge between staff and leadership. Whether you're interpreting employee feedback or crafting retention programs, HR must own its role as the expert in people management. This includes not just understanding the numbers but understanding people.

BE PART COACH, PART CHEERLEADER

Tony emphasizes that employees need to be heard and supported. HR professionals must guide employees through their journey at the organization while also celebrating their wins. The retention bonus plan at CNFA is a clear example of how organizations can cheer on their employees for their long-term commitment.

IGNITE THE SPARK

Engagement thrives when employees are passionate about their work. By listening to employees' needs, HR can inspire that passion. For Tony, sparking engagement meant focusing on workplace flexibility and trust in the post-Covid world, showing that employees' voices matter when making significant policy decisions.

BRING CLARITY FROM THE CLOUDS

One of Tony's most important messages was about transparency. Engagement efforts fall flat if employees don't understand how their feedback is being used or why certain decisions are made. Clear communication is the key to maintaining trust and demonstrating that their concerns are being addressed.

FORWARD AND ADAPTIVE BEATS STATIC AND SLOW

As the workplace evolves, so too must HR strategies. Tony's insights into the changing expectations of younger generations show that HR cannot rely on old-school thinking. By being forward-thinking and adaptive, HR can implement retention and engagement strategies that meet today's workforce demands.

Conclusion

In conclusion, Tony's perspectives are a reminder that employee engagement is not a one-size-fits-all approach, and it's certainly not something that can be managed passively. HR leaders need to be active listeners, transparent communicators, and most importantly, adaptable. Employee engagement directly affects every facet of the business, from retention to profitability. HR's role is to ensure that engagement strategies aren't just words on paper—they're embedded into the organization's culture and values. By taking the time to truly understand what employees need and acting on those insights, HR professionals can transform the workplace into a space where people want to stay, grow, and succeed.

Unique Retention Challenges: When Standard Solutions Don't Apply

While there are many tried-and-true strategies for retaining employees, sometimes standard solutions don't work. In these cases, we must think creatively and adapt our approaches to address unique retention challenges effectively.

When faced with challenges in retention, we must be adept at identifying and responding to the unique retention challenges that arise in our organizations. By understanding these challenges and developing tailored solutions, we can improve employee satisfaction, reduce turnover, and support our organization's long-term success. Let's discuss some of the unique retention challenges we may face and explore innovative strategies to address them.

Understanding Unique Retention Challenges

CHALLENGE 1: REMOTE WORKFORCE RETENTION

The Issue   With the rise of remote work, retaining remote employees has become a unique challenge. Remote workers may feel isolated, disconnected from the company culture, and have fewer opportunities for informal interactions with colleagues.

Solutions   To address this, you need to create a strong virtual community. Regular virtual team-building activities, online social events, and frequent communication can help remote employees feel connected. Additionally, providing remote employees with the necessary tools and resources to perform their jobs effectively and offering flexible work schedules can enhance their job satisfaction.

CHALLENGE 2: RETAINING HIGH-POTENTIAL EMPLOYEES

The Issue   High-potential employees often seek rapid career advancement and challenging projects. If their needs are not met, they may be poached or look for opportunities elsewhere.

Solutions   To retain high-potential employees, we must provide them with clear career paths, opportunities for professional development, and challenging assignments that align with their skills and aspirations. Regularly discussing career goals and creating individualized development plans can keep these employees engaged and committed to the organization.

CHALLENGE 3: ADDRESSING BURNOUT AND WORK–LIFE BALANCE

The Issue   Burnout is a significant retention challenge, especially in high-pressure environments. Employees who experience chronic stress and lack work–life balance are more likely to leave. You may also find that employees suffer from presenteeism.

Solutions   Implementing wellness programs, promoting a healthy work–life balance, and encouraging the use of vacation time are crucial steps in addressing burnout. Flexible working arrangements and providing mental health support can also help employees manage stress and improve their overall wellbeing.

CHALLENGE 4: RETENTION IN COMPETITIVE INDUSTRIES

The Issue   In highly competitive industries, employees often receive attractive offers from rival companies, making retention particularly challenging.

Solutions   To retain employees in competitive industries, we must focus on creating a compelling employee value proposition (EVP). Competitive compensation and benefits are important, but so are opportunities for growth, a positive work environment, and a strong organizational culture. Highlighting the unique advantages of working for your organization can help retain top talent.

CHALLENGE 5: RETAINING DIVERSE TALENT

The Issue   Retention of diverse talent can be challenging if employees feel they are not included or valued within the organization.

Solutions   Building an inclusive culture is essential for retaining diverse talent. This involves providing diversity and inclusion training, creating employee resource groups, and ensuring that all employees feel respected and valued. Additionally, fostering a culture of open dialogue and addressing any instances of bias or discrimination promptly can improve retention among diverse employees. I've also found that diverse candidates who relocate to your office for work can benefit from understanding resources in the community that help them feel at home. Sometimes it's not the work environment that causes diverse candidates to resign; instead it's the lack of feeling a connectedness with the community they live in.

Implementing Tailored Solutions

STEP 1: ASSESS THE UNIQUE NEEDS OF YOUR WORKFORCE
Start by conducting regular surveys and focus groups to understand the specific needs and challenges faced by your employees. Use this data to identify patterns and areas that require attention.

STEP 2: DEVELOP CUSTOMIZED RETENTION STRATEGIES
Based on the insights gathered, develop tailored retention strategies that address the unique challenges of your workforce. Ensure these strategies are flexible and can be adapted as needs change.

STEP 3: COMMUNICATE AND ENGAGE
Clearly communicate the initiatives and resources available to support employee retention. Engage employees in the process by seeking their input and feedback on retention strategies.

STEP 4: MONITOR AND ADJUST
Regularly monitor the effectiveness of your retention strategies through metrics such as turnover rates, employee satisfaction scores, and feedback. Be prepared to adjust your approach based on what is working and what isn't.

In summary, unique retention challenges require innovative and tailored solutions. Whether it's retaining remote workers, high-potential employees, or diverse talent, understanding the specific needs of your workforce is key. By implementing customized strategies and continually assessing their effectiveness, we can improve employee retention and support organizational success.

> I encourage you to evaluate the unique retention challenges within your organization and develop creative, tailored solutions to address them. By doing so, you can foster a more engaged, satisfied, and loyal workforce.

CASE STUDY EXERCISE
Engagement and Retention in Action

You are the HR Director at HealthPlus, a healthcare organization known for its commitment to patient care and employee wellbeing. Despite having a mission-driven culture, HealthPlus has recently experienced higher than usual turnover rates and lower employee engagement scores. Feedback from exit interviews and employee surveys indicates issues such as burnout, lack of career growth opportunities, and insufficient recognition. Your task is to develop a comprehensive strategy to address these issues, enhance employee engagement, and improve retention.

Please note: This case study is entirely fictitious. Any relationship to a real-world organization or person is entirely coincidental.

Task

Develop a detailed plan to address the engagement and retention challenges at HealthPlus. Your plan should identify key issues, propose targeted solutions, and outline steps to implement and monitor these solutions effectively.

Supporting Questions

- What are the primary factors contributing to employee disengagement and turnover at HealthPlus?

- How can you gather more detailed information to understand these issues better?

- What specific strategies can you implement to reduce burnout among employees?

- What initiatives can you implement to foster a positive and inclusive work environment?

- What metrics will you use to measure the effectiveness of your engagement and retention strategies?

Engagement Checklist: Maintaining High Employee Morale

Maintaining high levels of employee engagement and retention requires consistent effort and strategic actions. This checklist outlines daily, weekly, monthly, quarterly, and annual activities to help you manage and improve employee engagement and retention effectively.

Daily Activities

EMPLOYEE CHECK-INS

- Have informal conversations with employees to gauge their mood and gather feedback.
- Be available to address any immediate concerns or issues that employees may have.

RECOGNITION

- Acknowledge small achievements and contributions made by employees.
- Send thank-you notes or give verbal praise to show appreciation.

MONITOR ENGAGEMENT METRICS

- Review real-time data on employee engagement platforms to identify any immediate trends or issues.
- Track attendance and punctuality as indicators of engagement.

Weekly Activities

TEAM MEETINGS

- Hold regular team meetings to discuss ongoing projects, provide updates, and address any team concerns.
- Encourage open communication and solicit feedback from team members.

REVIEW EMPLOYEE FEEDBACK

- Analyze feedback from employee surveys, suggestion boxes, or other feedback mechanisms.
- Address any emerging issues and follow up with employees who provided feedback.

TRAINING AND DEVELOPMENT

- Schedule and conduct short training sessions or workshops on relevant topics.
- Encourage employees to share knowledge and skills with their peers.

CHECK PROGRESS ON GOALS

- Review the progress of team and individual goals set for the week.
- Provide guidance and support to help employees stay on track.

Monthly Activities

EMPLOYEE RECOGNITION PROGRAMS

- Implement monthly recognition programs to highlight outstanding performance and contributions.
- Celebrate employee milestones, such as work anniversaries and achievements.

ENGAGEMENT ACTIVITIES

- Organize team-building activities, social events, or wellness programs to foster a positive work environment.
- Encourage participation in these activities to build camaraderie and morale.

PROFESSIONAL DEVELOPMENT

- Offer training programs, workshops, and online courses to support employee growth and development.
- Review individual development plans and adjust as necessary.

ONE-ON-ONE MEETINGS

- Schedule monthly one-on-one meetings between managers and employees to discuss performance, goals, and career aspirations.
- Provide constructive feedback and discuss any concerns or suggestions.

Quarterly Activities

EMPLOYEE SURVEYS

- Conduct comprehensive engagement surveys to gather detailed feedback on employee satisfaction and engagement.
- Analyze survey results to identify trends and areas for improvement.

PERFORMANCE REVIEWS

- Conduct quarterly performance reviews to assess employee performance and provide feedback.
- Set new goals and development plans based on performance outcomes.

REVIEW ENGAGEMENT METRICS

- Analyze quarterly engagement metrics, such as turnover rates, absenteeism, and participation in engagement activities.
- Identify patterns and develop strategies to address any issues.

DIVERSITY AND INCLUSION INITIATIVES

- Review and enhance diversity and inclusion programs to ensure a welcoming and inclusive workplace.
- Organize events and training sessions to promote diversity and inclusion awareness.

STRATEGIC PLANNING

- Review and update engagement and retention strategies to align with organizational goals.
- Set specific, measurable objectives for the next quarter.

Annual Activities

COMPREHENSIVE ENGAGEMENT REVIEW

- Conduct a thorough review of the year's engagement and retention efforts.
- Evaluate the effectiveness of programs and initiatives and identify areas for improvement.

EMPLOYEE ENGAGEMENT SURVEY

- Conduct an annual comprehensive employee engagement survey to gather in-depth feedback.
- Use survey results to inform strategic planning and initiatives for the coming year.

RECOGNITION AND AWARDS CEREMONY

- Organize an annual awards ceremony to recognize outstanding achievements and contributions throughout the year.
- Celebrate employee successes and highlight the impact of their work.

TRAINING AND DEVELOPMENT PLAN

- Develop an annual training and development plan based on organizational needs and employee feedback.
- Allocate budget and resources for professional development opportunities.

POLICY REVIEW

- Review and update engagement and retention policies to ensure they reflect current best practices and organizational goals.
- Ensure compliance with legal and regulatory requirements.

STRATEGIC GOAL SETTING

- Set strategic goals for employee engagement and retention for the upcoming year.
- Align goals with the overall strategic objectives of the organization and allocate resources accordingly.

This checklist provides a structured approach to managing employee engagement and retention. By breaking down activities into daily, weekly, monthly, quarterly, and annual tasks, we can maintain consistency and drive continuous improvement.

I encourage you to integrate this checklist into your routine and customize it to fit your organization's needs. By doing so, you can enhance your engagement and retention practices and build a committed, motivated workforce.

Reflective Questions on Retention: Evaluating Your Practices

Retaining top talent and ensuring high employee engagement are essential pillars of organizational success. HR professionals must take a proactive approach to reflect on and refine their retention strategies. It begins with understanding what truly drives employee engagement. Is it clearly defined and measured in your organization, or is there ambiguity around its significance? More importantly, are you addressing the factors that influence engagement, such as meaningful work, strong communication, and opportunities for professional development?

Evaluating the effectiveness of current engagement strategies is vital. Ask yourself, which initiatives are working, and why? And for those that fall short, where do the gaps lie? Being transparent with employees about these reflections fosters a culture of continuous improvement. Equally essential is the topic of burnout and work–life balance. While engagement might be strong, if burnout levels are rising, employee wellbeing is being compromised. HR should consistently review the organization's approach to supporting work–life balance and stress reduction.

Career growth and development opportunities are central to long-term retention. Employees need to feel that their professional journey is supported, with clear paths to advancement. HR can expand its training and development programs to ensure employees feel empowered in their careers. Alongside development, frequent recognition is key. How often do we recognize employees' contributions, and do we recognize them in ways that resonate with their preferences?

Beyond individual initiatives, it's critical to assess the overall work environment. Would employees describe it as inclusive, supportive, and collaborative? HR must play a role in fostering such an environment, ensuring that every employee feels heard and valued. Effective leadership and communication are also cornerstones of engagement. Leadership accessibility and responsiveness are necessary to build trust and a sense of belonging among employees.

Regular feedback loops are essential. Seeking employee input on engagement and satisfaction helps HR stay ahead of challenges. More importantly, acting on this feedback and showing employees that their voices result in tangible changes strengthens trust and retention. Equally, diversity and inclusion efforts are a critical aspect of creating an engaging workplace. HR needs to continuously evaluate and improve diversity initiatives to build a truly inclusive culture.

One of the greatest retention challenges lies in understanding why employees leave. Exit interviews and surveys provide valuable insights that can guide HR in making necessary changes to improve retention. HR should also be open to exploring new and innovative engagement practices. The workplace is evolving, and so should our approaches. Whether it's utilizing new technology or adopting flexible work models, HR should lead the charge in experimenting with modern engagement strategies.

Finally, HR's retention and engagement efforts must align with the organization's overall goals. A clear alignment ensures that employees understand how their work contributes to the company's mission, reinforcing a sense of purpose and belonging. Monitoring and evaluating these efforts through concrete metrics allow HR to continuously track progress and make data-driven decisions.

By applying the five HR values—Own Your Expertise; Be Part Coach, Part Cheerleader; Ignite the Spark; Bring Clarity From the Clouds; and Forward and Adaptive Beats Static and Slow—HR can enhance employee engagement and retention strategies. Owning expertise means HR takes charge of these initiatives with confidence. Acting as a coach and cheerleader means HR both guides employees toward success and celebrates their achievements. Igniting the spark is about creating opportunities for growth and development that keep employees motivated. Bringing clarity ensures transparency in all communications, and being adaptive allows HR to stay agile, constantly refining its approach to meet the needs of a dynamic workforce.

By focusing on these values and continuously improving practices, HR can play a transformative role in building a workplace where employees feel engaged, valued, and motivated for the long term.

Regularly reflecting on these questions can help you identify strengths and areas for improvement in your engagement and retention practices. Use these insights to drive more effective and impactful strategies.

Conclusion

In conclusion, employee engagement is a continuous journey, not a one-time initiative. As HR leaders, we hold the key to shaping a work environment where employees feel connected, appreciated, and empowered. By applying the five core HR values, we ensure our engagement and retention strategies are not only effective but also aligned with the organization's broader goals. Remember, an engaged workforce isn't just more productive—it's a workforce that drives innovation, fosters loyalty, and builds long-term success. Now is the time to assess, refine, and commit to engagement strategies that resonate deeply with your team and support your organization's vision. Together, we can create a culture where every employee feels heard, supported, and motivated to contribute their best.

9

Company Culture

Introduction

In today's fast-paced business world, company culture is more than a buzzword—it's the bedrock upon which successful organizations are built. A thriving workplace culture is not merely a set of programs or policies; it's a living system that grows with the organization, touching every aspect of how we work. The importance of culture cannot be overstated—when effectively cultivated, it can drive employee engagement, boost retention, and set your organization apart from competitors.

In this chapter, we explore the transformative power of company culture and how HR leaders can leverage it to create a unified, dynamic, and high-performing workforce. Through practical examples and actionable insights, we'll examine how aligning culture with core business values can result in sustainable success, even in the face of global challenges. HR professionals have the unique power to shape these environments, turning culture into a competitive advantage that fuels both personal and organizational growth.

In our opening fictional story, we focus on Parker Enterprises, a global staffing agency where Chief People Officer Alan faces a daunting task: uniting the company's fractured culture across three different countries. As challenges surface and tensions rise, Alan introduces innovative programs that gradually transform the workplace. But can his efforts truly bridge the cultural gaps and bring lasting change?

Culture Counts: A Story of Transformation Through Culture

Alan Rogers, the Chief People Officer of Parker Enterprises, a staffing agency with operations in the U.S., U.K., and India, faced the challenge of transforming a fragmented company culture. The employee feedback he gathered revealed a lack of cohesion, inconsistent management, and varying levels of engagement across regions.

Determined to improve the culture, Alan launched a series of initiatives to unite employees and foster collaboration. He introduced "Culture Hubs," virtual meetings where staff from all regions could share experiences and connect, helping employees feel part of a global team. This initiative broke down regional silos and opened lines of communication.

Alan also implemented manager training programs, emphasizing empathy and cultural awareness. Managers were encouraged to act as culture ambassadors, leading their teams with a unified, people-first approach. Additionally, Alan introduced a flexible work policy that respected the specific needs of each region, ensuring employees felt supported and valued.

Within months, the changes began to show results. Employee engagement and satisfaction rose, while collaboration between the offices increased. Retention rates improved, and a stronger sense of shared purpose emerged across Parker Enterprises.

Through his focused efforts, Alan succeeded in creating a cohesive, inclusive company culture. His initiatives not only strengthened the company internally but also enhanced its global performance, positioning Parker Enterprises as a leading employer in the staffing industry. Alan's strategic focus on culture had a lasting, positive impact on both employees and the company's overall success.

Cultivating Culture:
Core Principles for an Invigorating Workplace

Cultivating a positive and invigorating workplace culture is not just a "nice-to-have"—it's essential for driving engagement, innovation, and long-term success. After all, employees don't fall in love with work by accident. There must be an intentional effort to create a place people enjoy working at.

As stewards of our organization's culture, it's our responsibility to ensure that it aligns with our values and strategic objectives. A strong, positive culture can enhance employee satisfaction, boost productivity, and attract top talent. Let's explore the core principles of cultivating a culture that invigorates and inspires our workforce.

Core Principle 1: Define and Communicate Your Values

IMPORTANCE OF CLEAR VALUES

Values are the foundation of any strong culture. They guide behaviors, decision-making, and interactions within the organization. Clearly defined values help employees understand what is expected of them and what they can expect from the organization.

STRATEGIES TO IMPLEMENT

Start by defining the core values that align with your organization's mission and vision. Communicate these values consistently through all levels of the organization. Incorporate them into your onboarding process, performance reviews, and daily communications. Use storytelling and real-life examples to illustrate how these values are lived out in the workplace.

Core Principle 2: Lead by Example

ROLE OF LEADERSHIP

Leaders set the tone for the entire organization. When leaders embody the values and principles they espouse, it reinforces those values throughout the organization. Conversely, a disconnect between leadership behavior and stated values can undermine trust and credibility.

STRATEGIES TO IMPLEMENT

Encourage leaders at all levels to model the behaviors and attitudes that reflect the company's values. Provide training and support to help leaders develop the skills needed to lead effectively. Regularly recognize and celebrate leaders who exemplify the desired culture. Ensure that leadership actions are transparent and aligned with organizational values.

Core Principle 3: Foster Open Communication

THE NEED FOR TRANSPARENCY

Open and transparent communication builds trust and fosters a sense of community. Employees who feel informed and heard are more likely to be engaged and committed to the organization.

STRATEGIES TO IMPLEMENT

Create channels for regular and open communication between employees and leadership. This can include town hall meetings, regular updates from senior leaders, and platforms for anonymous feedback. Encourage a culture where feedback is welcomed and acted upon. Ensure that communication is two-way, allowing employees to voice their ideas, concerns, and suggestions.

Core Principle 4: Empower Employees

EMPOWERMENT AND ENGAGEMENT

Empowering employees to take ownership of their work and make decisions fosters a sense of responsibility and engagement. When employees feel trusted and valued, they are more likely to contribute their best efforts.

STRATEGIES TO IMPLEMENT

Provide employees with the autonomy to make decisions related to their roles. Offer opportunities for professional development and career growth. Encourage innovation and creative problem-solving by giving employees the freedom to experiment and take risks. Recognize and reward initiative and leadership at all levels.

Core Principle 5: Build a Sense of Community

CREATING CONNECTIONS

A strong sense of community within the workplace enhances collaboration, loyalty, and overall job satisfaction. Building relationships among employees fosters a supportive and inclusive environment.

STRATEGIES TO IMPLEMENT

Organize team-building activities, social events, and volunteer opportunities to help employees connect on a personal level. Promote diversity and inclusion initiatives to ensure that all employees feel welcome and valued. Encourage cross-functional collaboration and the sharing of knowledge and resources. Celebrate successes and milestones together, reinforcing a sense of shared purpose and achievement.

In summary, cultivating a positive and invigorating workplace culture involves defining and communicating clear values, leading by example, fostering open communication, empowering employees, and building a sense of community. These core principles create an environment where employees feel valued, engaged, and motivated.

I encourage you to evaluate your current workplace culture and identify areas where you can implement these principles. By doing so, you can build a culture that not only supports your strategic objectives but also makes your organization a great place to work.

Mentor's Corner: Culture Is a System, Not a Program

In my conversation with Angela Howard, Founder of Call for Culture, we focused on how company culture is not just a set of programs but an ongoing system that evolves over time. Angela stresses that culture is formed by behaviors, values, and traditions reinforced by leadership and employees alike. Many companies historically misunderstood this concept, assuming that offering perks like ping-pong tables or free snacks was enough to build culture. But culture isn't shaped by those surface-level perks; it's shaped by behaviors, values, and a sense of shared purpose. When leadership and HR can successfully align their behaviors and values with the company's mission, that's when true culture is built.

One of the key takeaways from our discussion was how companies often approach culture with a programmatic mindset. They view culture as something you can add on, like an HR program. Angela explained that the most successful companies have shifted away from this model and now understand that culture operates like a system. It's about changing behaviors at every level, not just offering perks. The shift from focusing on cultural "add-ons" to an integrated, systemic approach means organizations are starting to understand that real culture change requires effort from everyone, particularly leadership.

Angela also emphasized the importance of context. Culture doesn't exist in a vacuum—it reflects broader societal changes. As HR professionals, we must acknowledge this reality and stop separating the workplace from societal issues. Whether it's race, gender equality, or even political and economic crises, these issues affect how employees show up at work. Culture, therefore, has to address not only the goals of the organization but also the concerns employees bring with them from the outside world.

One best practice Angela shared for building positive workplace culture is ensuring leadership alignment. When leadership isn't on the same page regarding what the company culture should look like, you create cognitive dissonance within the organization. Imagine having eight different executives all interpreting company values in different ways. That inconsistency will confuse employees and deteriorate trust in the company's culture. Instead, leadership must be aligned, not just on the values themselves but on what it looks like to live those values daily.

Accountability is another cornerstone of building great culture. You can't build culture if you don't have mechanisms to hold people accountable for behaviors that undermine it. Culture is like a garden, Angela told me. If you don't weed out toxic behaviors, they'll kill the culture you're trying to cultivate. It's not enough to create values; you have to actively protect them by removing people or behaviors that harm the company's environment.

Finally, culture is shaped from the bottom up, not just from the top down. Leaders need to involve employees in defining what culture means at every level. Employees are the ones experiencing the day-to-day of the workplace, so their input is critical. This doesn't mean letting employees dictate everything, but it does mean co-creating the culture by including their feedback and lived experiences.

When we talked about aligning culture with business strategy, Angela shared how vital it is to have a well-defined, clear business strategy that inspires and motivates people. If your business strategy is just a to-do list for the year, you won't rally your people around it. A great business strategy should connect with employees emotionally and show them how their work contributes to the larger goals of the company. From there, your culture-building initiatives should breathe life into that strategy. Leaders need to invest in these initiatives with real time, energy, and resources. If employees sense that culture initiatives are only for show, they will disengage.

Technology also plays a big role in shaping culture today. Angela highlighted how technology can actually create more human-centered experiences by freeing up HR's time for more strategic tasks. When HR leaders are bogged down by administrative tasks like payroll or onboarding, they can't focus on more meaningful cultural work. By leveraging technology, we can streamline these processes and dedicate more time to building a thriving company culture.

In terms of future trends, Angela believes HR professionals will need to develop two critical skills. First, the ability to have tough conversations—whether about societal issues, employee concerns, or conflicts in the workplace. Employees today want their companies to take a stance on important issues, and HR needs to lead those discussions. Second, HR professionals need to become futurists. We need to be better at reading societal signals and predicting how they will impact our workplaces. The work implications that came along with the Covid-19 pandemic and the Great Resignation were both events that caused many HR leaders to be proactive on behalf of their organizations.

Angela also shared some of the challenges she faces when working with companies on culture change. Often, the root of cultural issues lies with one or two key leaders who are setting the wrong tone for the organization. This lack of self-awareness at the top makes it difficult to move forward with real culture change. But by assessing a company's readiness for change upfront and holding leaders accountable throughout the process, we can make real progress.

Applying the Five HR Values

Now, let's tie these insights to the five HR values we've discussed throughout the book.

OWN YOUR EXPERTISE

Angela's insights remind us that HR professionals must step into their roles as cultural architects. We need to go beyond program management and lead culture-building efforts that shape behavior across the organization.

BE PART COACH, PART CHEERLEADER

Culture change isn't easy. HR must guide leaders and employees through the ups and downs, coaching them to embrace new behaviors while also celebrating their progress.

IGNITE THE SPARK

True culture transformation starts with a vision that excites people. Just as Angela described the need for a motivating business strategy, HR must light the spark that gets people excited about the culture they're helping to build.

BRING CLARITY FROM THE CLOUDS

Culture can be an abstract concept, but HR's role is to clarify it. We need to make culture tangible by setting clear expectations, aligning leadership, and creating accountability mechanisms.

FORWARD AND ADAPTIVE BEATS STATIC AND SLOW

Culture is always evolving, and HR needs to stay ahead of the curve. We must be adaptive, forward-thinking, and ready to guide our organizations through the cultural shifts that come with societal change.

Conclusion

Angela's perspective on culture challenges us to think bigger about what it takes to build and sustain a thriving company culture. It's not about perks or programs; it's about shaping behaviors, holding people accountable, and aligning culture with the broader business strategy. By embracing the power of culture as a system, we can create workplaces that are not only productive but also deeply fulfilling for the people who work there.

Culture Pitfalls: Navigating Toxic Workplace Culture

Every HR professional will at some point confront toxic workplace culture. A toxic culture can erode employee morale, productivity, and ultimately, the success of an organization. Recognizing and remedying these cultural pitfalls is essential for creating a healthy, thriving work environment.

As senior HR leaders, it is our duty to identify the signs of a toxic culture and implement strategies to address and rectify them. By proactively managing these issues, we can transform our workplaces into environments where employees feel valued, respected, and motivated. Let's delve into the common pitfalls that lead to a toxic workplace culture and discuss effective strategies for navigating and overcoming them.

Pitfall 1: Poor Leadership and Management

THE ISSUE

Leadership sets the tone for the entire organization. When leaders display toxic behaviors such as favoritism, lack of transparency, micromanagement, or neglect, it trickles down and affects the entire workforce.

STRATEGIES TO NAVIGATE

Invest in leadership development programs that emphasize emotional intelligence, ethical behavior, and effective communication. Provide regular feedback and coaching to leaders. Encourage a leadership style that is transparent, inclusive, and supportive. Hold leaders accountable for their actions and ensure they are modeling the values and behaviors expected in the organization.

Pitfall 2: Lack of Respect and Inclusion

THE ISSUE

A workplace where employees do not feel respected or included can quickly become toxic. Discrimination, harassment, and exclusionary practices create a hostile environment.

STRATEGIES TO NAVIGATE

Promote a culture of respect and inclusion through comprehensive diversity and inclusion training. Implement clear policies against discrimination and harassment, and ensure they are enforced consistently. Create channels for employees to report concerns safely and confidentially. Foster an environment where diverse perspectives are valued and everyone feels they belong.

Pitfall 3: Ineffective Communication

THE ISSUE

Poor communication can lead to misunderstandings, mistrust, and a lack of cohesion among employees. When information is not shared transparently, or when communication is dismissive or condescending, it contributes to a toxic culture.

STRATEGIES TO NAVIGATE

Develop and implement a robust communication strategy that promotes transparency, openness, and inclusivity. Encourage regular, two-way communication between employees and management. Provide training on effective communication skills for all employees. Utilize multiple platforms to ensure that important information is accessible to everyone.

Pitfall 4: Unmanageable Workloads and Burnout

THE ISSUE

Employees who are consistently overworked and stressed are at high risk of burnout, which can contribute to a toxic work environment. Unrealistic expectations and lack of support exacerbate this issue.

STRATEGIES TO NAVIGATE

Monitor workloads and ensure they are manageable. Promote work–life balance by encouraging the use of vacation time and flexible working arrangements. Provide resources for stress management and mental health support. Regularly check in with employees to gauge their workload and wellbeing, and make adjustments as necessary.

Pitfall 5: Lack of Recognition and Reward

THE ISSUE

Employees who feel undervalued and unappreciated are more likely to disengage and contribute to a negative work environment. A lack of recognition and reward can lead to feelings of resentment and demotivation.

STRATEGIES TO NAVIGATE

Implement a comprehensive recognition and rewards program that acknowledges employees' efforts and achievements. Ensure recognition is timely, specific, and meaningful. Solicit feedback from employees on how they prefer to be recognized and rewarded. Celebrate successes, both big and small, to boost morale and foster a positive culture.

In summary, navigating and addressing a toxic workplace culture involves improving leadership and management practices, fostering respect and inclusion, enhancing communication, managing workloads to prevent burnout, and recognizing and rewarding employees effectively. By tackling these issues head-on, we can transform our workplace culture into one that is healthy, supportive, and productive.

> I encourage you to assess your organization's current culture and identify any signs of toxicity. Implement the strategies we've discussed to address these issues and create a positive, thriving work environment.

CASE STUDY EXERCISE
Toxic Leadership Overhaul

You are an HR Director at GreenTech Innovations, a company committed to environmental sustainability. The CEO, John, has been with the company since its inception and has played a significant role in its growth. However, his leadership style and certain outdated management practices have contributed to a toxic workplace culture. John is open to change, but finds it challenging to break away from his old ways. Your task is to develop a strategy to help John transform the culture at GreenTech Innovations into a positive and productive environment.

Please note: This case study is entirely fictitious. Any relationship to a real-world organization or person is entirely coincidental.

Task

Develop a comprehensive strategy to address the toxic elements of the workplace culture at GreenTech Innovations. Your strategy should focus on helping John adopt new leadership practices, improving overall workplace culture, and ensuring that the changes are sustainable.

Supporting Questions

- How can you gather detailed information about these issues from employees and other stakeholders?

- What leadership development programs can you recommend to help John and other leaders at GreenTech Innovations improve their leadership styles?

- How can you enhance communication between John, the leadership team, and employees to build trust and transparency?

- What mechanisms can you implement to ensure that employees feel heard and valued?

- What initiatives can you introduce to foster a positive and inclusive work environment?

Culture-Building Checklist: Key Activities for Leaders

Building a positive company culture requires consistent and deliberate actions from leadership.

If your company is already a great place to work then give your department a collective pat on the back, but don't let up on your efforts. Your role in impacting workplace culture is to ensure the organization's people, systems, and approach to work remain optimal. As a senior member of the HR department in your organization, you will want to make sure you have a structured way to evaluate programs, quantify the results, and make improvements to keep things in tip-top shape.

Daily Activities

MODEL POSITIVE BEHAVIOR

- Leaders should demonstrate the organization's values through their actions and decisions.
- Encourage open and respectful communication among employees.

ENGAGE WITH EMPLOYEES

- Have informal check-ins with team members to show genuine interest in their wellbeing and work.
- Address any immediate concerns or issues raised by employees.

RECOGNIZE CONTRIBUTIONS

- Acknowledge small achievements and efforts made by employees.
- Provide immediate and specific feedback to reinforce positive behavior.

Weekly Activities

TEAM MEETINGS

- Hold regular team meetings to discuss progress, challenges, and goals.
- Encourage team members to share their ideas and feedback.

CROSS-DEPARTMENTAL COLLABORATION

- Facilitate opportunities for employees from different departments to collaborate on projects.
- Promote knowledge sharing and teamwork across the organization.

EMPLOYEE FEEDBACK

- Review feedback received from employees through various channels.
- Address any recurring themes or urgent issues promptly.

Monthly Activities

RECOGNITION PROGRAMS

- Implement a monthly recognition program to highlight outstanding performance and contributions.

- Celebrate employee milestones such as work anniversaries and personal achievements.

PROFESSIONAL DEVELOPMENT

- Offer training sessions, workshops, and webinars to support employee growth.
- Review individual development plans and adjust them as needed.

DIVERSITY AND INCLUSION INITIATIVES

- Organize events and activities that promote diversity and inclusion.
- Encourage participation in employee resource groups (ERGs) and related initiatives.

Quarterly Activities

EMPLOYEE SURVEYS

- Conduct comprehensive engagement surveys to gather detailed feedback on the workplace culture.
- Analyze survey results to identify trends and areas for improvement.

PERFORMANCE REVIEWS

- Conduct quarterly performance reviews to assess employee progress and provide feedback.
- Set new goals and development plans based on performance outcomes.

CULTURE AUDIT

- Review and assess the current state of the workplace culture.
- Identify any gaps or areas that need improvement and develop action plans.

TEAM-BUILDING ACTIVITIES

- Organize team-building exercises and social events to strengthen relationships and foster a sense of community.
- Encourage participation to enhance team cohesion and morale.

Annual Activities

STRATEGIC PLANNING

- Review and update the organization's cultural goals and strategies for the upcoming year.
- Align cultural initiatives with overall business objectives.

COMPREHENSIVE CULTURE REVIEW

- Conduct a thorough review of the year's cultural initiatives and their effectiveness.
- Evaluate the impact on employee engagement, retention, and overall performance.

LEADERSHIP TRAINING

- Provide advanced leadership training programs to develop and enhance leadership skills.
- Focus on areas such as emotional intelligence, inclusive leadership, and change management.

POLICY REVIEW

- Review and update organizational policies related to culture, diversity, and inclusion.
- Ensure policies reflect best practices and legal requirements.

ANNUAL RECOGNITION CEREMONY

- Host an annual awards ceremony to recognize and celebrate outstanding achievements and contributions throughout the year.

- Highlight success stories and reinforce the organization's values.

This checklist provides a structured approach to building and maintaining a positive workplace culture. By breaking down activities into daily, weekly, monthly, quarterly, and annual tasks, we can ensure consistency and drive continuous improvement.

> I encourage you to integrate this checklist into your routine and customize it to fit your organization's needs. By doing so, you can enhance your workplace culture and create an environment where all employees feel valued and motivated.

Culture Reflections: How Does Your Organization Measure Up?

When reflecting on your organization's culture, it's essential to consider both the broad strokes and finer details that make up the workplace environment. Culture isn't static; it's a living, evolving system that HR must continually nurture and assess. Are your core values clearly articulated and woven into the daily actions of leadership and employees alike? This alignment between values and behaviors is the foundation of strong culture, and HR plays a vital role in ensuring that these values aren't just words on paper but are lived experiences. Leadership, in particular, sets the tone for the entire organization. When leaders model the expected behaviors, it reinforces the importance of culture, making it easier for others to follow suit. Conversely, if leadership falls short, it weakens trust and undermines the desired culture.

Employee engagement is another pillar that HR should prioritize. Employees need to feel valued, included, and respected. How are you promoting diversity and inclusion? It's not enough to have policies in place—there must be visible, ongoing efforts that employees can see and feel. Equally important is communication. Open dialogue between employees and leadership fosters trust and transparency, but it must be a two-way street. Are you giving employees ample opportunity to provide feedback, and, more importantly, are you acting on it? Feedback should lead to tangible improvements, and HR has a responsibility to communicate those changes clearly to the workforce.

Recognition and rewards are integral to reinforcing culture. Employees need to feel their contributions are appreciated, and rewards should be meaningful to them, not just aligned with what the company deems valuable. Tied to this is work–life balance, which remains a critical issue. HR must ensure that wellbeing initiatives support not just productivity but also mental and emotional health. Burnout can rapidly erode a positive culture, so proactive measures, such as stress management programs and flexible work options, must be in place.

Professional development is equally vital to both culture and retention. Employees are more likely to stay with an organization if they see a path for growth. Do your training programs align with the aspirations of your workforce, and are they designed to address not only current needs but also future opportunities? Alongside development, collaboration and teamwork are key. How well do different departments work together? Barriers to effective collaboration can stunt cultural growth, and HR must actively identify and resolve these issues to foster a unified workplace.

Retention is often a reflection of culture. If employees are leaving, it's crucial to understand why. Conduct exit interviews, track patterns, and adjust your retention strategies accordingly. Sometimes cultural challenges can push employees away, but those same challenges present opportunities for improvement. Whether it's addressing inclusion gaps or reshaping leadership practices, culture can be continuously strengthened with the right attention.

Measuring cultural impact is where HR's role as a strategist becomes clear. Metrics such as employee engagement scores, turnover rates, and feedback mechanisms help track progress, but they must be aligned with the organization's strategic goals. Are your cultural initiatives sustainable? Can they withstand shifts in leadership or market conditions? HR must ensure that these efforts are deeply ingrained in the organization, so they endure over time.

Lastly, continuous improvement is critical. Culture is never "finished." It's a dynamic process that must evolve with both the internal and external environments. HR should remain vigilant, constantly seeking out new strategies and technologies to keep culture responsive and aligned with the organization's changing needs.

In conclusion, HR's power lies in shaping, nurturing, and sustaining a culture that is not only reflective of the company's values but also resilient in the face of challenges. By applying the five core HR values—Own Your Expertise; Be Part Coach, Part Cheerleader; Ignite the Spark; Bring Clarity From the Clouds; and Forward and Adaptive Beats Static and Slow—HR can build a thriving organizational culture that aligns with both employee needs and strategic objectives.

Regularly reflecting on these questions can help you gain a deeper understanding of your organization's culture and identify areas for improvement. Use these insights to drive meaningful and positive changes within your workplace.

Conclusion

As HR professionals, we hold the key to shaping the very essence of our organizations—its culture. This chapter has shown how deeply rooted cultural values and behaviors can influence not only the workplace environment but the long-term success of the organization. From fostering inclusivity and open communication to aligning with strategic goals, culture serves as the heartbeat of any thriving business. When leaders and HR teams are aligned on their vision for culture and equipped with the right tools and strategies, the potential for positive impact is limitless. The work we do to cultivate culture today will not only enhance employee wellbeing and engagement but will also create a lasting legacy that positions our organizations for sustained success.

Let's continue to challenge ourselves to be forward-thinking, adaptive, and intentional in building a culture that resonates with both employees and business objectives. The power of HR lies in our ability to lead these cultural transformations—driving change, fostering unity, and ensuring that every employee feels empowered and valued in the workplace.

10

Diversity, Equity, Inclusion, and Belonging (DEIB)

Introduction

In Chapter 10 of *The Power of HR*, we delve deep into the transformative power of diversity, equity, inclusion, and belonging initiatives. Organizations today must embed these principles not only into their strategic goals but into their everyday operations. To begin, understanding the gaps and strengths in your current DEIB efforts is key to driving progress. By evaluating the alignment of these initiatives with your mission, leaders can create workplaces where all employees feel valued, respected, and empowered. In this chapter, you'll find a roadmap to assess your current practices and elevate DEIB within your organization.

Let's jump into the topic with our fictional story. At Jordan Cookware USA, Chief Diversity Officer Glenda Jean embarks on a mission to transform the company's culture by enhancing its DEIB efforts. Through employee councils, mentorship programs, and aligning diversity with business strategy, she creates a workplace where every voice is valued. Change starts with listening—impact follows.

Diverse Beginnings: Stories of Inclusion and Its Impact

Glenda Jean had been with Jordan Cookware USA for just over six months when she realized the company's DEIB efforts needed serious attention. As Chief Diversity Officer, she had always believed that true progress in DEIB wasn't just about numbers or compliance—it was about creating a culture where every employee felt valued and had the space to thrive.

The challenge at Jordan Cookware was both unique and pressing. With manufacturing plants in three states and a workforce that ranged from corporate executives to factory workers, the company had pockets of diversity, but inclusivity lagged. Employees from underrepresented groups often felt isolated, and although Jordan Cookware prided itself on being a family-owned business with strong values, there was little cohesion around how those values should translate into day-to-day inclusivity.

Glenda's first order of business was to listen. She visited each plant, sitting down with employees to understand their experiences. In a small-town Arkansas factory, she met Laura, a production line worker who had been with the company for fifteen years. Laura spoke about feeling disconnected from the company's broader goals and how, as a woman in a male-dominated environment, she often felt her voice went unheard. Similar sentiments were echoed by employees across all levels—whether they worked in logistics in Texas or marketing in Illinois.

Determined to make a meaningful impact, Glenda set out to change the narrative. She knew that creating a truly inclusive culture wouldn't happen overnight, but she believed that if employees saw leadership's commitment to change, they'd be willing to contribute.

Her plan began with a bold step: establishing DEIB councils at each plant, composed of a diverse mix of employees. These councils were tasked with identifying specific, localized issues and brainstorming actionable solutions. They became the eyes and ears of DEIB efforts on the ground, helping Glenda gain real insights into the challenges faced by different teams.

She also launched a mentorship program that paired senior leaders with employees from underrepresented backgrounds, helping them navigate their careers while fostering cross-level understanding. One of the first participants, a Latina engineer named Ana, had always felt that her career had plateaued. After just three months of mentorship, Ana felt more empowered and confident in her leadership potential, crediting her mentor's support and guidance for her renewed motivation.

Glenda understood that DEIB couldn't be just another corporate initiative—it had to be woven into the very fabric of Jordan Cookware. She worked closely with the CEO, Dorothy Jordan, and the executive team to align DEIB with the company's strategic objectives. Together, they restructured their hiring and promotion processes, ensuring that bias-reducing tools like blind resume reviews and diverse interview panels became the standard.

One year later, the results were beginning to show. Employee satisfaction scores rose, turnover rates dropped, and, most importantly, there was a palpable shift in the culture. Laura, who had once felt overlooked, was now leading a cross-functional team to improve production processes. Ana had been promoted to a leadership role within her engineering division, a visible testament to the company's commitment to inclusive growth.

Glenda's work wasn't done—she knew the journey toward true inclusion was ongoing. But seeing the change firsthand, she felt a sense of accomplishment. By creating space for every voice at Jordan Cookware, Glenda helped the company build not just better cookware but a stronger, more united workforce.

The DEIB Imperative: Why Diversity Isn't Just an Option

Diversity, equity, inclusion, and belonging are essential components for building a thriving workplace. This isn't just a people-centric mantra for us as HR professionals to grasp, it's a truth that must be codified in the very fabric of our organizations from top to bottom. And for good reason. Not only do diverse teams improve innovation, drive financial performance, and help teams make better decisions, there are external factors that organizations must adapt to in the changing landscape of business. The impact of the DEIB imperative reaches across several core aspects of the business: legal and ethical imperatives, employee engagement and retention, and customer and market relevance.

As senior HR leaders, it is our responsibility to champion DEIB initiatives within our organizations. By understanding and embracing the importance of diversity, we can create workplaces that are not only equitable and inclusive but also thrive in today's competitive landscape. Let's discuss the critical reasons why DEIB must be at the forefront of our strategic priorities.

Diversity Drives Innovation

THE POWER OF DIVERSE PERSPECTIVES

Diversity brings a wealth of different perspectives, experiences, and ideas to the table. When people from varied backgrounds collaborate, they challenge each other's assumptions and spark creativity. This leads to innovative solutions and approaches that a homogenous group might not have considered.

REAL-WORLD EXAMPLES

Consider how diverse teams at companies like Google and Apple have driven groundbreaking innovations. These organizations recognize that diverse perspectives are key to staying ahead in a rapidly evolving market. By fostering diversity, we can ensure our teams are more innovative and better equipped to solve complex problems.

Enhanced Decision-Making

DIVERSE TEAMS MAKE BETTER DECISIONS

Diverse teams make better decisions. They are more likely to consider a wider range of options and potential outcomes, leading to more effective and well-rounded solutions.

PRACTICAL INSIGHTS

When people from different backgrounds collaborate, they bring unique insights that help identify risks and opportunities more comprehensively. This diversity of thought leads to more robust and effective decision-making processes.

Improved Financial Performance

THE BUSINESS CASE FOR DIVERSITY
Organizations that prioritize DEIB tend to outperform their peers financially. Diverse companies are more likely to attract top talent, understand and serve diverse customer bases, and enter new markets successfully.

ORGANIZATIONAL SUCCESS
By embracing diversity, companies not only enhance their performance but also gain a competitive edge. The ability to tap into diverse markets and customer bases drives growth and sustainability.

Attracting and Retaining Talent

THE WORKFORCE OF THE FUTURE
Today's workforce values diversity and inclusion. Millennials and Gen Z, who make up a significant portion of the labor market, seek employers who are committed to DEIB principles. Organizations that fail to prioritize DEIB risk losing out on top talent to more inclusive competitors.

CREATING AN INCLUSIVE ENVIRONMENT
By fostering a culture where all employees feel valued and included, we can improve employee satisfaction, reduce turnover, and build a loyal and engaged workforce. This not only benefits individual employees but also enhances organizational performance and resilience.

Social Responsibility and Brand Reputation

BUILDING A POSITIVE BRAND

In today's socially conscious world, organizations are increasingly held accountable for their DEIB practices. Consumers, investors, and stakeholders are more likely to support companies that demonstrate a genuine commitment to diversity and inclusion.

ENHANCING BRAND REPUTATION

By actively promoting and practicing DEIB, we can build a positive brand reputation, enhance customer loyalty, and attract socially conscious investors. This, in turn, drives long-term success and sustainability.

In summary, the imperative of DEIB is clear. Diversity drives innovation, enhances decision-making, improves financial performance, attracts and retains top talent, and builds a positive brand reputation. As HR leaders, it is our responsibility to champion these principles and integrate them into every aspect of our organizations.

> I encourage you to evaluate your current DEIB initiatives and identify areas for improvement. Let's commit to making diversity, equity, inclusion, and belonging integral to our organizational strategies and daily practices.

Mentor's Corner: You Can Do Good and Do Well at the Same Time

In my conversation with Adonica Black, Senior Director of Global Talent, Inclusion and Employee Brand at Adaptiv, we explored the evolving role of DEIB in the modern business landscape. Adonica emphasizes that DEIB is not just a buzzword or an initiative—it's an accelerator for business success. Her core belief is simple yet powerful: You can do good and do well simultaneously. The organizations that figure this out are the ones that will thrive in the future.

As wealth shifts from Baby Boomers to younger generations like Millennials and Gen Z, businesses need to align with the values of these groups. They care deeply about diversity and inclusion, and they're making decisions with their dollars. To build a "future-ready" company, it's essential to embrace DEIB, not just in theory but in everyday practice.

Adonica points out that one of the biggest challenges in DEIB is resistance to change, whether it stems from unconscious bias or political ideology. However, she stresses that educating leaders on the direct business benefits of inclusion is crucial. She engages them by quantifying the impact of DEIB on business outcomes—showing how inclusivity drives innovation, engagement, and overall financial performance. Leaders must own their expertise and champion DEIB in every room, ensuring the initiatives move beyond surface-level efforts. This is how organizations bring clarity from the clouds—by tying abstract values to concrete outcomes.

Middle managers, who feel the operational pressures the most, present a unique challenge. They often need guidance on how to integrate DEIB into their day-to-day roles. Adonica helps these managers realize that inclusive hiring practices, such as reaching out to diverse talent pools, can meet their pressing need to fill positions while also improving team dynamics. This is where the value of being part coach, part cheerleader comes in. Middle managers need support to navigate these complexities, but they also need encouragement to see how inclusion aligns with their goals.

At the individual contributor level, fostering an environment where employees feel valued and heard is crucial. Adonica is working to create platforms where employees can share their experiences and feedback. This helps managers bring clarity from the clouds, as they better understand what's happening on the ground and how to address it.

The most rewarding part of this work, Adonica says, is seeing the direct impact on people. She describes a leadership development program where several employees have already been promoted, thanks to the tailored support they received. This is what it means to ignite the spark—identifying talent, nurturing it, and watching it flourish.

Adonica shared several best practices that have proven successful in fostering DEIB. Structured interviews, for example, ensure that all candidates go through the same process, reducing bias and creating a more equitable hiring experience. Clear job descriptions that focus on essential skills help avoid excluding diverse talent who may not meet every single requirement but have the potential to grow into the role. By owning their expertise, hiring managers can better identify and develop talent within their teams.

Onboarding is another critical touchpoint. Ensuring that all new hires receive clear objectives, development opportunities, and support helps them integrate more effectively into the company culture. It's about being forward and adaptive rather than static and slow. Creating a consistent and equitable onboarding experience ensures that every employee has the tools they need to succeed from the very beginning.

Looking ahead, Adonica is excited about the potential of AI to eliminate bias in areas like resume screening and job descriptions. She's also exploring how AI can help employee resource groups enhance engagement and measure the effectiveness of their programs. This focus on innovation aligns with the value of being forward and adaptive. It's about leveraging technology not just to streamline processes but to create more human-centered, inclusive experiences.

Adonica also highlights the need for DEIB practitioners to prepare for increased reporting and compliance requirements. As DEIB becomes a more central business function, there's a growing demand for transparency and accountability. HR professionals must bring clarity from the clouds by ensuring that their practices are well-documented and in compliance with emerging regulations.

Wellbeing is another area where Adonica sees growing importance. Post-pandemic, there's a renewed focus on employee wellness, and DEIB practitioners must pay particular attention to how burnout and mental health challenges affect diverse communities. Supporting employees' wellbeing is not just about offering perks—it's about creating an inclusive environment where everyone can thrive.

In terms of measuring the success of DEIB initiatives, Adonica's approach is both quantitative and qualitative. She tracks demographic representation, retention rates, promotion rates, and employee engagement scores. However, she also looks at the qualitative feedback from surveys and focus groups to understand the deeper nuances of employee sentiment. These insights are then shared with leaders to help them drive meaningful improvements in their departments.

Applying the Five HR Values

OWN YOUR EXPERTISE

HR professionals must be confident in their ability to guide their organizations through complex DEIB challenges. Leaders and managers rely on HR's expertise to navigate these waters, and owning that expertise is key to driving success.

BE PART COACH, PART CHEERLEADER

Support managers and leaders in their DEIB efforts by providing both guidance and encouragement. Help them see how inclusion can drive better business outcomes while offering the tools to achieve it.

IGNITE THE SPARK

Identify and nurture talent within your organization. Whether through leadership development programs or inclusive hiring practices, HR has the power to ignite the potential in every employee.

BRING CLARITY FROM THE CLOUDS

Use data and insights to tie abstract concepts like diversity and inclusion to concrete business outcomes. Help leaders understand the impact of DEIB on performance, retention, and engagement by providing clear, actionable metrics.

DEIB isn't a one-time initiative—it's a continuous process that requires agility and innovation. Embrace new tools like AI and stay ahead of trends to ensure your DEIB efforts remain relevant and effective.

Conclusion

My conversation with Adonica underscored the importance of making DEIB a core part of business strategy. By integrating these principles into every level of the organization—from leadership to individual contributors—companies can not only do good but also do well. Through the application of the five HR values, HR professionals can play a pivotal role in creating future-ready organizations that thrive on diversity, equity, inclusion, and belonging.

Challenges in DEIB: Addressing Uncommon Complexities

While DEIB initiatives are essential, they often come with unique and complex challenges. These challenges truly are circumstantial because not every organization is the same. On one hand, you will find very progressive organizations that fully embrace DEIB initiatives and have a strong culture of employees bringing their full selves to work. On the other, you have organizations that err on the side of homogeny and choose the familiar instead of branching out across the various plains of diversity.

Companies find themselves on various ends of the DEIB-readiness spectrum, but so do individuals. In a 2023 Pew Research survey, 56 percent of adults surveyed said that focusing on increasing diversity, equity, and inclusion at work is mainly a good thing. The narrow minority of respondents (16 percent) said that it is a bad thing. The ambivalent middle 28 percent said it is neither good nor bad (Minkin, 2023).

Let me ask you a question… If you had to think about 100 people in your organization, where would your leadership team fall? What about line managers? How about lay employees? As HR professionals, we face the daunting task of not only seeking DEIB buy-in at the macro level, we must understand that every individual has their own perspective about the topic.

Here are some of the most common hurdles we face when attempting to adopt and sustain DEIB initiatives across the organization.

Resistance to Change

Resistance to change is a challenge we've all encountered at some point, whether it be for DEIB initiatives or otherwise. You're excited about rolling out a new DEIB program, but not everyone shares your enthusiasm. It's disheartening to hear grumblings of skepticism from your team or doubts from the leadership.

I have found that the root of resistance can take shape in many forms. Sometimes organizational leaders are not convinced that investment in DEIB is better than the status quo. Think of the CEOs who believe the most important datapoint is the bottom-line revenue and who already have their own levers they like to pull to make the number bigger. Another form of resistance can be the biases we hold about one another—whether that be informed by our religious views, where we grew up, the media sources we consume, or even our socio-economic status. I could go on about other root causes of resistance, but that is not the point. The point is that all resistance has some anchoring belief. The sooner you can tap into the limiting belief, the sooner you can establish common ground and make progress towards the goal of lasting adoption of DEIB efforts.

A well-thought-out change management strategy can help you and your organization overcome resistance in a way that is both methodical and strategic. Begin by first getting a sense of what beliefs stand in the way of embracing your change fully. Next, clearly communicate the benefits of DEIB initiatives in meaningful and persuasive terms, not only for company culture but also for business success. Share data and case studies that highlight how diversity fuels innovation and boosts the bottom line. There are several resources listed at the end of this chapter that will help you accomplish this goal.

Implement mandatory education and training sessions to underline the importance of diverse perspectives. By aligning DEIB efforts with the company's goals, you can gradually win over the skeptics and ease the transition.

Unconscious Bias

If we can be honest, we all have unconscious bias about people who differ from us. That can make diversity initiatives tough to implement because not only are you trying to convince your staff to change their actions, you're asking for many to change their beliefs. Aiming for equal pay amongst men and women? What about the team members who believe women don't work as hard as men? Trying to increase minority hiring in management positions? What about the team members who feel they are inherently more qualified than minority candidates regardless of their inferior credentials?

Unconscious bias is the invisible whisperer who keeps us stuck in our ways because we believe the worst, or differently, about others. It must be addressed if you want progress because it can creep into our decisions and interactions, subtly influencing outcomes in ways we might not even realize.

SCENARIO

You notice a pattern where, despite having a diverse pool of candidates, certain groups consistently land the jobs and promotions. It's a sign that unconscious bias might be at play in the recruitment and advancement processes.

SOLUTION

To combat this, start with comprehensive bias training for everyone involved in hiring and promotions. Introduce blind recruitment techniques, removing names and other identifying details from resumes during initial screenings. This helps ensure candidates are assessed solely on their skills and experience. Over time, these measures can help create a fairer, more inclusive environment where everyone has a genuine opportunity to succeed.

Cultural Differences

In today's global workplace, understanding and respecting cultural differences is crucial. However, it's not always easy to navigate these nuances.

SCENARIO

Picture this: you manage a team spread across different regions. You notice that what works communication-wise in one area causes misunderstandings in another. For example, a direct communication style in one location might be seen as harsh in another.

SOLUTION

Cultural competence training is key here. Educate your team about the various cultures represented in your organization to foster understanding and respect. Additionally, celebrate these diverse cultures through events and initiatives where employees can share their traditions and customs. This approach promotes inclusivity and helps build a cohesive, harmonious work environment where cultural differences are valued.

Inclusion Fatigue

While DEIB initiatives are vital, it's possible to push too hard and too fast, leading to inclusion fatigue where employees feel overwhelmed.

SCENARIO

After several months of intensive DEIB activities—workshops, training sessions, panel discussions—you start noticing a decline in enthusiasm. Employees begin expressing that the continuous focus on DEIB is exhausting and overwhelming.

SOLUTION

Balance is crucial. Integrate DEIB initiatives seamlessly into the overall organizational strategy instead of treating them as separate efforts. Ensure these initiatives are balanced with other business priorities and provide support through mental health resources and wellness programs. This approach helps maintain engagement and enthusiasm without causing burnout.

Measuring DEIB Impact

One of the toughest parts of implementing DEIB initiatives is measuring their impact. It's essential to quantify success to demonstrate value and secure ongoing support.

SCENARIO

You've rolled out several DEIB programs, but when it comes to proving their effectiveness, you find it challenging to show concrete results. Without clear metrics, it's hard to justify further investment.

SOLUTION

Establish clear metrics and KPIs to track progress and outcomes. Measure factors such as employee engagement, retention rates, and the diversity of candidate pools and leadership teams. Regularly report these metrics to illustrate the positive impact of DEIB efforts. This transparency helps secure continued support from stakeholders by demonstrating tangible benefits.

Conclusion

Implementing effective DEIB initiatives is no small feat, but it's crucial for creating a thriving and dynamic workplace. By developing robust strategies, providing comprehensive training, and measuring the impact of your efforts, you can overcome these common challenges. Remember, each step you take towards a more inclusive and equitable workplace makes a significant difference. Let's continue to champion DEIB together!

CASE STUDY EXERCISE

Enhancing Workplace Inclusion for Remote Employees

You are the HR Director at TechWave, a company that has recently transitioned to a hybrid work model with a significant portion of the workforce working remotely. Despite the flexibility this model offers, remote employees have reported feeling disconnected and excluded from important conversations and decisions. The CEO, Alex, is eager to improve the experience for remote employees but needs guidance on how to create a more inclusive and engaging remote work culture. Your task is to develop a strategy to address these issues and foster a sense of belonging among remote employees.

Please note: This case study is entirely fictitious. Any relationship to a real-world organization or person is entirely coincidental.

Task

Develop a detailed plan to enhance inclusion and engagement for remote employees at TechWave. Your strategy should focus on identifying key issues, proposing targeted solutions, and outlining steps to implement and monitor these solutions effectively.

Supporting Questions

- What specific challenges are remote employees facing in terms of inclusion and engagement?

- What communication strategies can you implement to ensure remote employees feel included and informed?

- What initiatives can you introduce to create a stronger sense of community among remote employees?

- What metrics will you use to measure the success of your inclusion and engagement initiatives for remote employees?

- How will you track progress and make adjustments to your strategy based on feedback and data?

DEIB Checklist: Consistent Practices for Inclusivity

Creating a diverse, equitable, inclusive, and belonging workplace requires consistent and intentional efforts. This checklist outlines daily, weekly, monthly, quarterly, and annual activities to help you manage and improve your DEIB initiatives effectively.

Daily Activities

MODEL INCLUSIVE BEHAVIOR

- Demonstrate inclusive behavior in all interactions and decision-making processes.
- Encourage and practice open and respectful communication with all employees.

ENGAGE WITH EMPLOYEES

- Have informal check-ins with team members to show genuine interest in their wellbeing and experiences.
- Be available to address any immediate concerns or issues related to DEIB.

RECOGNIZE CONTRIBUTIONS

- Acknowledge the efforts of employees who contribute to creating an inclusive environment.
- Provide immediate and specific feedback to reinforce positive behavior.

Weekly Activities

TEAM MEETINGS

- Hold regular team meetings to discuss DEIB initiatives and progress.

- Encourage team members to share their ideas and feedback on DEIB matters.

CROSS-DEPARTMENTAL COLLABORATION

- Facilitate opportunities for employees from different departments to collaborate on DEIB projects.
- Promote knowledge sharing and teamwork across the organization.

REVIEW FEEDBACK

- Analyze feedback received from employees through various channels regarding DEIB.
- Address any recurring themes or urgent issues promptly.

Monthly Activities

RECOGNITION PROGRAMS

- Implement a monthly recognition program to highlight contributions to DEIB efforts.
- Celebrate diverse employee milestones and achievements.

PROFESSIONAL DEVELOPMENT

- Offer DEIB training sessions, workshops, and webinars to support employee growth and awareness.
- Review individual development plans with a focus on DEIB goals.

DIVERSITY AND INCLUSION INITIATIVES

- Organize events and activities that promote diversity and inclusion.
- Encourage participation in employee resource groups and related initiatives.

Quarterly Activities

EMPLOYEE SURVEYS

- Conduct comprehensive DEIB surveys to gather detailed feedback on the workplace culture.
- Analyze survey results to identify trends and areas for improvement.

PERFORMANCE REVIEWS

- Conduct quarterly performance reviews with a focus on DEIB goals and achievements.
- Set new DEIB-related goals and development plans based on performance outcomes.

DEIB AUDIT

- Review and assess the current state of DEIB initiatives.
- Identify any gaps or areas that need improvement and develop action plans.

TEAM-BUILDING ACTIVITIES

- Organize team-building exercises and social events to strengthen relationships and foster a sense of community.
- Encourage participation to enhance team cohesion and morale.

Annual Activities

STRATEGIC PLANNING

- Review and update the organization's DEIB goals and strategies for the upcoming year.
- Align DEIB initiatives with overall business objectives.

COMPREHENSIVE DEIB REVIEW

- Conduct a thorough review of the year's DEIB initiatives and their effectiveness.
- Evaluate the impact on employee engagement, retention, and overall performance.

LEADERSHIP TRAINING

- Provide advanced DEIB training programs to develop and enhance leadership skills.
- Focus on areas such as emotional intelligence, inclusive leadership, and change management.

POLICY REVIEW

- Review and update organizational policies related to DEIB.
- Ensure policies reflect best practices and legal requirements.

ANNUAL RECOGNITION CEREMONY

- Host an annual awards ceremony to recognize and celebrate outstanding achievements in DEIB throughout the year.
- Highlight success stories and reinforce the organization's commitment to DEIB.

This checklist provides a structured approach to managing DEIB initiatives. By breaking down activities into daily, weekly, monthly, quarterly, and annual tasks, we can ensure consistency and drive continuous improvement.

> I encourage you to integrate this checklist into your routine and customize it to fit your organization's needs. By doing so, you can enhance your DEIB efforts and create an inclusive, equitable, and engaging work environment.

Reflective Inquiry: Assessing Your DEIB Efforts

When assessing your organization's DEIB efforts, it's essential to start with clear goals that align with your company's mission. DEIB initiatives should not exist in isolation; they must be woven into the fabric of your organizational values. This means clearly defining DEIB goals and communicating them at every level, from leadership to individual employees. Leaders must not only talk the talk but demonstrate a commitment to inclusion by taking concrete actions that reflect DEIB values.

One key consideration is representation. Does your workforce mirror the diversity of the communities you serve? This isn't just about checking boxes—it's about making sure that diversity is visible at all levels of the organization, from entry-level positions to leadership roles. Alongside this, ensuring that your hiring, promotion, and retention practices are truly inclusive is vital. Employees should have equal opportunities for advancement, regardless of their background, and this is where HR plays a crucial role in aligning processes with DEIB principles.

Training and education also play a significant role in fostering an inclusive workplace. Ongoing DEIB training ensures that both leaders and employees are culturally competent and aware of unconscious biases. These efforts must be paired with active ERGs that provide platforms for diverse employee voices, while also helping to create spaces of belonging. But inclusion goes beyond formal policies—leaders need to ignite the spark by fostering a workplace where all employees feel engaged and valued.

Addressing bias and discrimination is essential. A robust policy to address complaints and ensure a respectful work environment should be non-negotiable. Additionally, gathering employee feedback on DEIB efforts is crucial for continuous improvement. The feedback loop brings clarity from the clouds, as it helps HR to make data-driven decisions that reflect the lived experiences of employees and foster genuine belonging.

HR leaders must be part coach, part cheerleader, encouraging managers to implement these inclusive practices and own their expertise in advancing DEIB goals. They should also ensure that DEIB initiatives are not short-term projects but sustainable practices integrated into daily business operations. Celebrating diversity, acknowledging contributions, and forming strong external partnerships are further strategies that can advance the DEIB agenda.

Ultimately, measuring the impact of DEIB initiatives is crucial. This includes tracking progress through metrics like representation, retention, and employee engagement. Aligning DEIB efforts with strategic goals and ensuring they are sustainable for the long term will solidify DEIB as a core business imperative that drives innovation, belonging, and success for all employees.

> Regularly reflecting on these questions can help you gain a deeper understanding of your organization's DEIB practices and identify areas for improvement. Use these insights to drive meaningful and positive changes within your workplace.

Conclusion

At the core of this journey is the role of HR professionals. We must act as both coaches and cheerleaders, guiding teams through DEIB challenges while celebrating progress. Owning your expertise is critical when implementing these initiatives, while being forward-thinking and adaptive ensures DEIB efforts remain relevant. Through fostering inclusivity, HR leaders ignite a spark in employees, encouraging them to bring their whole selves to work. Ultimately, clarity is brought from the clouds when DEIB practices are consistently measured, ensuring progress and long-term impact.

Reference

Minkin, R (2023) Diversity, Equity and Inclusion in the Workplace, Pew Research Center, www.pewresearch.org/social-trends/2023/05/17/diversity-equity-and-inclusion-in-the-workplace/ (archived at https://perma.cc/N5MK-M28L)

Conclusion

As you finish reading *The Power of HR*, it's essential to reflect on the journey you, the reader, have embarked on through the previous chapters. You've explored the full spectrum of human resources, from talent management to diversity, equity, inclusion, and belonging (DEIB), employee engagement, and strategic workforce planning. But now, as we wrap up this comprehensive journey, it's time to remember that HR is not just a function—it's a driving force of organizational success.

First, let me congratulate you for reaching this point. Reading this book was no small task. You've absorbed key insights and strategies that will shape your career as an HR professional. You've delved into practical examples, thoughtful reflection questions, and learned the critical role HR plays in steering an organization toward its goals. Keep in mind that the lessons in this book are not just theoretical— they are actionable. The power of HR lies in its ability to transform organizations and enhance the lives of employees, and now you hold the tools to do just that.

Throughout the book, we've discussed five foundational HR values that are crucial to your success:

1 **Own Your Expertise:** HR professionals are experts in their field, but that expertise only carries weight when it's applied confidently. Whether navigating complex compliance issues, implementing DEIB strategies, or driving leadership development, owning your expertise ensures you have a seat at the strategic table.

2 **Be Part Coach, Part Cheerleader:** As HR leaders, we are both mentors and motivators. Our role is to guide employees and celebrate their successes while challenging them to reach their potential. Whether it's through talent development, performance management, or supporting leaders, this value embodies the supportive nature of HR.

3 **Ignite the Spark:** Engagement doesn't happen by accident. Whether through employee recognition, innovative DEIB initiatives, or clear development pathways, HR is responsible for sparking motivation and ensuring employees are inspired to perform their best.

4 **Bring Clarity From the Clouds:** HR often deals with ambiguity. Whether it's navigating complex situations like employee grievances or translating strategic goals into workforce plans, HR professionals bring clarity and provide direction when things are uncertain.

5 **Forward and Adaptive Beats Static and Slow:** In today's fast-paced business environment, HR must stay ahead of the curve. You've learned how crucial it is to remain agile, adapting to change, and fostering a culture of continuous learning and improvement. These attributes help keep your organization dynamic and future-ready.

Now, as you move forward in your HR career, think of *The Power of HR* as your roadmap. You've gained tools, strategies, and frameworks that will help you build stronger, more inclusive workplaces. Whether you're shaping culture, managing talent, or guiding leadership development, remember that the power to influence change lies within your grasp.

HR is a vital part of any organization's success. From fostering innovation through diverse teams to ensuring employees feel valued, respected, and engaged, HR professionals are the catalysts for growth. You have the ability to drive impact, not just by filling roles but by shaping the future of your organization.

In conclusion, the journey doesn't end here. Use this book as a reference guide throughout your career, coming back to its pages whenever you face new challenges or need inspiration. The world of

HR is constantly evolving, and staying grounded in these principles will ensure you remain effective and influential. Remember, you can always do well by doing good—prioritize people, drive business outcomes, and let the power of HR shape the future.

Thank you for trusting *The Power of HR* to be part of your professional journey. I'm excited for the positive change you'll create in your organizations. The future is yours to shape, and the power is in your hands.

INDEX

Looking for another book?

Explore our award-winning books from global business experts in Human Resources, Learning and Development

Scan the code to browse

www.koganpage.com/hr-learning-development

More from Kogan Page

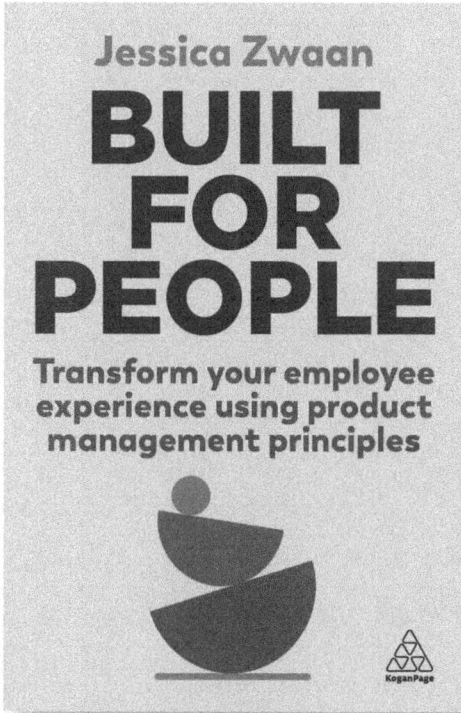

Jessica Zwaan

BUILT FOR PEOPLE

Transform your employee experience using product management principles

ISBN: 9781398608023

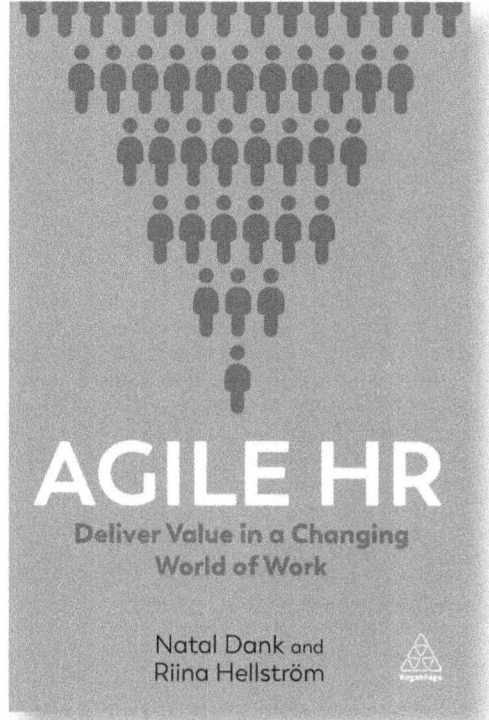

AGILE HR

Deliver Value in a Changing World of Work

Natal Dank and Riina Hellström

ISBN: 9781789665857

www.koganpage.com